PRAISE FOR *THE BEAU*

'In *The Beauty Load*, Nicole Mathieson ge[...] of mirrors that is the modern pressure to be [...] question how much of our precious time and energy is invested in keeping the 'shoulds' of how we look satiated, we become blind to our own true, deep beauty within. If you have ever questioned where external expectations of beauty end, then read this book. *The Beauty Load* strips everything back to remind us that it isn't what we look like that matters but how connected we are to ourselves and those we cherish.'
—Lauren White, Confidante to Women in Power and author of *Permission: Personal liberation for switched-on women*

'Nicole's raw personal journey and compelling professional insight have come together in the most spectacular way in *The Beauty Load*. The wisdom within is a call to inner freedom and deeply unconditional self-love. Nicole shines a light on the factors contributing to our deflated self-image and inner doubt, and guides us towards a more truly beautiful way. It's time we heed this profound message and love ourselves relentlessly.'
—Kris Franken, spiritual wayshower and author of *The Call of Intuition*

'*The Beauty Load* shines a hard-hitting light on what so many women (myself included!) have been hugely impacted by, but never had the words—or the courage—to express. Through her use of beautifully interwoven personal stories, Nicole normalises the unexpressed internal battles the Beauty Load causes and the detrimental impacts it has, and teaches us how to shift our relationship with ourselves and our bodies. *The Beauty Load* isn't just for the woman who wants to love her physical self more; it will improve your intimate relationships, friendships, and sense of self, and help you milk all of the richness that life has to offer. This book is packed full of heart-hitting *ahas* that will fill you with a deep sense of inspiration, empowerment and relief.'
—Che Johnson, soulful copywriter for heart-centred businesswomen

'This is a much-needed book, and I will certainly recommend it to my clients. As I read it, I was flooded with warmth for Nicole, for myself and for all women who suffer with the Beauty Load. The Beauty Load is inescapable really, isn't it. I can't imagine any woman who doesn't experience it. The book is very accessible, easy to read and motivating. Nicole writes in a warm and engaging manner.'
—Anne Moorhouse, psychologist and author of *Not Forgotten: They called me Number 10 at Neerkol Orphanage*

The
Beauty
Load

HOW TO FEEL ENOUGH IN A WORLD OBSESSED WITH BEAUTY

NICOLE MATHIESON

The Beauty Load

HOW TO FEEL ENOUGH IN A WORLD OBSESSED WITH BEAUTY

the kind press

This publication contains the opinions and ideas of its author. It is intended to provide helpful and informative material on the subjects addressed in the publication. While the publisher and author have used their best efforts in preparing this book, the material in this book is of the nature of general comment only. It is sold with the understanding that the author and publisher are not engaged in rendering advice or any other kind of personal professional service in the book. In the event that you use any of the information in this book for yourself, the author and the publisher assume no responsibility for your actions.

Disclaimer: The journey towards accepting your body is an individual one, and as such, the author is unable to guarantee that you will feel any different after reading this book. Any change requires commitment, courage and action. This book does not offer professional advice. If you are triggered, concerned or having catastrophic thoughts, please consult a doctor, psychiatrist or psychologist for professional advice for physical and/or mental matters.

Many of the stories in this book are heteronormative in nature. This is due to the author's exposure and experience rather than a reflection of the extent or limitations of the Beauty Load. The stories are used as examples, and relatable no matter what your identity and gender. All names and identifiable details of the individuals in this book have been changed to protect their privacy.

Cover design: Mila Cover Designs
Editing: Georgia Jordan
Internal design: Nicola Matthews, Nikki Jane Design

Cataloguing-in-Publication entry is available from the National Library Australia.

NATIONAL
LIBRARY
OF AUSTRALIA

ISBN: 978-0-6453444-3-1
ISBN: 978-0-6453444-4-8 (ebook)

This book is inspired by and written for all the women in my community—which, as you are reading these words, includes you—many of whom have had the courage to share their struggles and let me in to their 'shameful' thoughts, or have supported me as I have grappled with my own. You have all given me the permission to see my own load for what it really is.

This book is dedicated to our beautiful bodies. It is a granting of permission for me and you to let go of the struggle, feel confident about who we are in the world, and trust that we are worthy of connection with others, with pleasure and with ourselves—regardless of how we look.

Thus, this book is also for our children. It is my offering to change the insanity in our culture around looks and beauty, even in the smallest way. My wish is that we can all stand in our value for all that we are. My wish is that, while we all (our children included) might doubt our looks, we will know that the doubt is an expected stepping stone to something deeper and more beautiful.

The Beauty Load was conceived and written on Yuggera and Turrbal lands. I acknowledge and respect the Traditional Custodians of the land and waters on which I live and work and recognise their continuing connection to land, water and community. I pay my respects to Elders past, present and emerging.

Contents

Part III   **HOW DO WE GET OUT FROM**
             UNDERNEATH THE BEAUTY LOAD?

Beauty is truth, truth beauty, – that is all
Ye know on earth, and all ye need to know.

Ode on a Grecian Urn, 1820, John Keats

Introduction

Have you ever felt insecure about how you look?

Have you ever thought that you had to change or fix the way you looked in order to be loved?

If you are a woman, then I am imagining, due to the world around you, that you are replying yes to these questions. This book is written for you and every other woman like you who has ever felt inadequate due to the way she looks.

As you may have guessed, my own answer to those questions—as the author of a book called *The Beauty Load*—is 'Yes, yes, a resounding yes.' And if you're anything like me, the notion of beauty, or the perceived lack of it, may make you feel unworthy. Sometimes, it may even have the power to make you feel like you don't belong, or at worst, like you are not worthy of being loved. It is not uncommon for women to feel insecure about how they look. Think about all the women you know, and I'm sure you will agree.

Some of us may have gone to post a filter-free selfie but then felt disgusted by our face. Some of us may have felt like we can't leave the house without make-up on, or like we had to cover ourselves up during sex because we felt scared to be truly seen. Others among us may even have gone so far as to opt out of life—not going to the party; not speaking out about what's important to us; not going for the job opportunity; saying no to fun adventures, the beach or a relationship possibility—all because we didn't feel confident in the way we looked.

If you can relate, let me introduce you to something that I call the Beauty Load, a cultural and societal pressure that makes us look at others in comparison and feel like we're not good enough.

The Beauty Load is an invisible load of tension, an almost constant undercurrent of worry about how we are perceived, or sense of lack relating to how we look. It's a feeling that ebbs and flows through different phases and contexts of our lives, but in one way or another always seems to be sitting on our shoulders, taking up precious space in our mind and in our life that would be best used for … well, literally anything else.

Just like that mental load we carry around with us about what needs to be done at work, with the kids and around the house, the Beauty Load burdens us with yet more unending things to think about, only this time it's about our face, our hair, our clothes, our body, our … beauty.

Do I have the right clothes to wear to that event?

Am I going to look fat in the photos?

Should I wear heels so I look a little taller or go with comfy flats, even though I know I'll feel dumpy?

What will they think of me looking like this?

Is my boyfriend looking at that beautiful woman?

We have these and many other questions circulating in our heads all the freaking time.

Always wondering if we are beautiful enough has the power to make us feel anxious and to take away our self-worth, which sounds kind of ridiculous when we say it out loud. If we are completely honest with ourselves (and that is what I'll ask you to be as you read this book), these thoughts have been circulating in our heads for most of our lives and creating all kinds of internal havoc that have stopped us from living our lives as fully as possible.

As we'll explore, the Beauty Load comes from many places and is ever-present in our lives, and yet, it is so insidious and ingrained in our culture and our thinking that many women don't even realise that they are being negatively impacted by it; instead they believe what they are feeling is due to their own faults and imperfections. The Beauty Load feels personal.

I can imagine that you might turn to the author photo of me at about this point (if you haven't done it already). You might want to check out my beauty 'credentials' and see where I fit on the 'ideal beauty' hierarchy. Maybe you will look at the way I look and think, *What would she know about the struggles of not looking beautiful? She's tall, slim and white. She's not got a clue.* Or maybe you will think, *I get it, being a freckle-faced redhead with a flat chest must have offered her a few body image challenges.* Maybe you will look and think *She looks like the kind of woman I can trust* or maybe you'll think the opposite. All of this is okay. All of this is normal. All of this is the Beauty Load.

Part of the Beauty Load is the very natural instinct of judging what we see at face value—an important way that we keep ourselves safe. But another part, and the part that I am suggesting is a problem, is the comparison and judgement that the Beauty Load encourages. This part makes us judgemental and critical of others and, more detrimentally, ourselves. And the point of this book is not about whether you and I are at different places on the 'beauty ideal' hierarchy. The point is that we both, we **all** feel the Beauty Load, because of the way our culture has conditioned us.

The Beauty Load is subtle, yet pervasive. You may not know that it is weighing heavily on your shoulders until you get away from it. For me, this occurs when I take a camping trip into the wilderness. For you, it may be different; perhaps when you spend time alone or in the company of someone with whom you know you are safe to truly be yourself. If, like me, you have the inclination to get out into the wild, you will find yourself communing only with nature—the trees, the campfire, some trusted friends and stars above—and here, your whole system can relax. You can breathe and feel your body from the inside, rather than perceive it from the way it looks on the outside. For a moment, you feel the delicious lightness of being free from the Beauty Load.

In the wilderness, you are one with nature and it inescapably draws you back into being one with *your* nature. With you. *The you that I call the Self*—that is a functioning, whole, big-hearted being filled with the life, feelings and desires that make you you.

Without the influence of culture and the media telling you that you should be something else, and without a mirror to provoke your own judgemental parts, you can sit in the peaceful understanding that there is nothing 'not enough' about you. You feel different; better about yourself. In nature, this is your normal. But then, inevitably, you come back to 'real life'— to society, work, community and exposure to the culture, the images, the comparison—and the Beauty Load is there waiting for you to climb back in under its weighted canopy, where you are comfortable and familiar, albeit burdened.

In the warped, beauty obsessed, marketing-fuelled society that we live in, feeling the Beauty Load is normal. Thinking we are faulty and our bodies are the problem is how we adapt successfully to living in this culture. The culture is flawed. The Beauty Load and the way it makes us feel is its legacy.

Do you feel different when you are in nature?
If not, what are the conditions that help you escape
the burden of the Beauty Load?

While the world creates the conditions for the Beauty Load within us, the good news, if there is any, is that you are not alone, you and your body are not the problem, and there is relief available for us.

To feel relief from the impacts of the Beauty Load, we need to really see the realities of its impact on ourselves personally and as a culture. This book aims to first expose the negativity and personal impact of the Beauty Load and then light the way to easing it by pointing you back to your own values and capacity for self-compassion. The key here is that, in order to better deal with the Beauty Load, we need to first acknowledge this invisible, constant pressure that we carry, and see it as separate from the way we see ourselves.

Feeling the Load is understandable; it makes sense that we have this negativity and that we are really worried about fitting in (because, in our society, fitting in really, bloody matters). When we offer ourselves and others compassion instead of criticism and judgement, the fear softens and we can start to really change our inner culture, which is the first step towards changing the culture of the world that created the Beauty Load in the first place.

Being open and honest about the Beauty Load will help ease the pressure on us and its hold over us because, when we keep it to ourselves, the Beauty Load feels shamefully personal. It is not. We all feel it, no matter how much we are perceived to align with the agreed-upon beauty ideals of the day. When we think that our sense of inadequacy is personal—i.e. a result of our own particular beauty flaws and faults—then we keep the struggle to ourselves, we are compelled to fix and change ourselves externally and we feel our self-worth and value clinging to the surface fix or dwindling away.

The more we scroll through social media and have airbrushed grabs of perfect lives and bodies to compare ourselves against, the more we are going to feel it. My aim is for you to know (and I will repeat many times throughout this book) that you feeling insecure about your looks is not a reflection of your particular looks, but of the culture you have been raised in.

This book aims to raise awareness of the personal, emotional and psychological toll that the Beauty Load takes on us. It also examines the connection between the Beauty Load and our intimate relationships. How does our struggle to hold ourselves and our bodies as valuable affect our dating lives and intimate relationships? And lastly, this book offers some ideas about how to lessen the weight of the Beauty Load for you and those around you.

Before we get into it, it's important to note that I write this book from a heterosexual, cisgender female perspective, as that is my experience as well as the experience of many of my clients and thus what I feel able to write about with expertise. But the Beauty Load is not limited to heterosexual cis women. In fact, the Beauty Load gets harder the further from the agreed-upon and idealised cultural beauty 'norm' you are. The negative impact of the Beauty Load does not discriminate, and this book is relevant no matter your sex, gender or orientation. However, the way you experience the Load will vary depending on your influences, culture and experiences.

To explore the impact of the Beauty Load and how to ease it, this book is divided into three parts.

First, what is the Beauty Load and where does it come from? In Part I of this book, we will get clear on what the Load is, the myths and beliefs about beauty that we have been burdened with, and where the Load comes from. You will see the Beauty Load in all its self-esteem-stealing nastiness, and as a result you will hopefully feel less burdened by the heavy weight of it.

Secondly, what is the Beauty Load doing to us? In Part II, we will look at all the ways the Beauty Load is making us feel 'less than'—the ego control; the lack of confidence; the warped perception of ourselves that makes us feel like we need to hide, buy more or fix ourselves. First we will explore the effects it is having on us internally, and then we will explore how it is affecting our intimate relationships and dating lives.

Thirdly, how can we get out from under it? In Part III, we will look at what we can do about the Beauty Load. I will share with you how I got out from under the Load in relation to my small breasts. Then we will explore some of the approaches that have worked for my clients. And I will share a compassion-based approach you can use with the Beauty Load that will have more long-lasting impacts than simply trying to 'love your body more'.

Part I

The Beauty Load: What it is and where it comes from

Chapter 1

The tissue tit trick

One night, aged sixteen, I was out with a few friends at a party—a party that we had heard about on the grapevine, not our usual crew or neighbourhood. Exactly the kind of party that made me feel extra nervous and shy, especially around the boys. On this night, however, as I stood there surrounded by the intoxicating surge of teenage hormones, I could sense that I was holding myself just a bit taller. I nearly felt confident.

The reason for this confidence boost was that I had breasts.

Not real breasts, but tissue ones.

Getting ready, I had folded up a wad of tissues for each cup and shoved them down my bra. The decision to wear them had been laboured over in front of my bedroom mirror for quite some time. It had me swinging like a pendulum from *Yes, I'm doing this—I look great!* to *No, I can't—what if someone found out?*

In the end, I had taken the risk and the tissues remained wedged in my bra. Push-up bras were yet to enter my realm, so these tissues were my own push-up invention, aimed at making me feel less conspicuous with my flat chest.

Despite the padding upping my cup size, I was nervous. There were so many things that could go wrong:

- The tissue could poke out over the top of my blouse

- I could lose one breast entirely and be all lopsided
- I could hook up with a guy and be found out if he dared to reach for my chest
- I could be outed by my girlfriends, confused by my sudden breast growth

BUT I DECIDED THE RISK WAS WORTH IT

For many of my adolescent and early adult years, I really wanted a boyfriend. I wanted love. Looking back now, I realise that what I really wanted was acceptance; to be seen and valued for who I was. But I had decided, years earlier, that I wasn't 'enough' (i.e. acceptable) as I was.

I thought that to be 'enough', I needed to be different. Specifically, I thought I needed bigger breasts. This belief, over the years, infected the way I held myself in the world and interacted socially, the way I responded to people, the treatment I put up with from potential suitors, and the romantic choices I made.

On this night, it was a relief to feel that I could hold myself differently.

I REMEMBER LOVING HOW I LOOKED WITH 'BREASTS'

These wads of tissues made me feel noticeably better about myself. Here I was at this party, hanging out—for maybe the first time—like I belonged. I felt that connections with other interested teens, particularly young men, might just be possible. Were others noticing how great my figure was with breasts? Or was the difference all in my head?

A few years later, my underwear drawer would hold a

collection of push-up bras. Some of them ultra-mega-lift versions, some with a whole fillet of slimy, cold breast to insert. The result would be a 'nice-sized' breast sitting on my flat chest and making me look, in a slightly weird way, like I had a B-cup. I always knew, however, that it did not look realistic. For a start, my pseudo-breasts sat on the wrong part of my body and made me look kind of warped.

The pull to change the way I looked, and the confidence boost that came with the change, was me experiencing the Beauty Load.

The Beauty Load had me conflicted. I wanted to fit in, so I hid or enhanced the parts of myself that were 'less than perfect', but instead of the changes making me feel a clean sweep of confidence and beauty, the aftermath was tinged with shame, fear and guilt as I grappled with the cover-up. I felt a fraud. I could be found out for not being a 'natural' beauty. Deep inside me, there was more shame; I was sending the message to my inner being that *I needed to change to be okay*. I would repeat this message over and over to myself for many years to come, cementing the idea that I was not okay in this body as it was, or who I was as a person. My inner being, *my loving Self,* knew that this was not right.

I stuck to enhancing my cup size for the next two decades as a way to feel better about myself. I knew the appeal of wanting to change myself to feel pretty and attractive. I knew the tangible confidence boost it gave me. For me, confidence pivoted around breast size. For you, it may be some other body part or feature that makes you feel different. But whatever it is, I bet that you have felt an internal pull to change. This is the Beauty Load.

Chapter 2

Not feeling pretty enough

BEING IN A POSITION TO CONSIDER THIS PRESSURE I AM CALLING THE BEAUTY LOAD IS A PRIVILEGE.

Worrying about how we look and whether we fit in is only possible when we are not in serious crisis. There are refugees fleeing their countries; people living in war-ravaged cities; people who are facing immediate environmental collapse; and those existing in poverty, abuse or neglect. For them, worrying about fitting in through the way they look is probably not top of mind. They are too busy focussing on their own and their loved ones' survival. The Beauty Load is a privilege experienced by those of us who have space enough in our psyche to look up and out beyond immediate survival needs and notice the pressure to belong in the world around us. It is this privilege that sometimes makes us feel ashamed for feeling it at all.

I am privileged in every way possible aside from my gender. I grew up not having to worry, for the most part, about money, safety, comfort, care, nourishment, racism, or opportunities in life. The way I looked was a big part of this: white, able bodied, cisgendered, heterosexual, tall and slim. I was able to walk through life and fit in, my possibilities bolstered by the way I presented. My advantage was that I looked similar enough to the people portrayed on TV, in ads and in the media.

I knew the way we look causes internal angst, but I don't think I realised that looks can create serious problems, a lack of fitting in, discomfort or even danger for people. But hang on a second—if I pause to think about it for a moment, I probably did realise others must have struggled more than me. I realised this because I noticed that others were different. I remember my younger self staring at people who looked different, while my mother hurried me along so as not to make a scene. But I'm afraid to say that in my little bubble of safety, the issue didn't impact me, and therefore I didn't think too much about it. That, in its essence, is privilege.

PAUSE FOR A MOMENT AND REFLECT
Did you grow up worrying that your looks could
create a problem, discomfort or danger?
What was your privilege?
What was your beauty privilege?

Don't get me wrong: even with this privilege, I still struggled (hard) with the Beauty Load. One of the messages of this book, in fact, is that the Beauty Load impacts all of us, regardless of our race, size, gender, ability, etc. But as we will discuss in Chapter 8, the less beauty privilege we have, the harder the Load can be.

A BIT ABOUT ME

I grew up in the 1970s and 80s in suburban middle-class Sydney. My upbringing was nourishing and sociable. However, Christian, moral, social, class and family values were loaded onto my and my friends' shoulders from all directions; we were taught to work hard, be nice and always, always look our best. We grew up with Benny Hill, *Porky's*, blonde jokes, homophobia, racism, sexism and old white men newsreaders with pretty young assistants. All of this of course helped cultivate the Beauty Load we've all felt since we were young.

The message that 'women need to be beautiful' was a constant foundation of the way families, culture and our society worked. I heard this message loud and clear as a young girl. It started with the message that boys' education was more important than girls' and kept going with ideas such as the pretty girls got the boyfriends and were more popular at school; that women should diet and try to be skinny; that beautiful women could marry 'well' and be financially looked after; and that only the beautiful, young women would get jobs in the public eye, as without the looks, nobody would want to see them on screens.

My friends and I knew from a very young age that our looks mattered, a lot, and we groomed and pruned ourselves to be validated in this world as much as we could.

The most validating thing of all was being found attractive by others. I wanted boys to find me attractive, peers to find me attractive, the aerobics class teacher, the random stranger, the adults in my life … pretty much everyone. There was a reward for being attractive and for fitting the beauty ideal, which started as praise as cute little girls and morphed into gawps from horny teens, but was encompassed by the comforting blanket of acceptance.

ACCEPTANCE

Acceptance. That is all we ever want. And it makes sense, as acceptance feels good. Acceptance is safety. Acceptance is comforting. We would all—to varying degrees at different stages of our lives—do what we needed to do in order to be accepted. We would play the game, tweak our own nature, say the words, become the person, do whatever … until we realised that being someone we are not is hard work and is not rewarding, because we are not really, truly being accepted for who we are. For our Self.

When it comes to our looks, we have been conditioned and primed to offer our acceptability up for appraisal. Do others find me attractive? Do they approve of my outfit? Do they let me in? We let the judges that be—our peers, the critics, the random men who glance our way—have the power. We hand this power over with the hope of belonging, which leaves us anxious, and self-scrutinising.

Over the years, we have scrutinised ourselves so much that it has become a habit that switches our own loving eyes into harsh judgemental ones. Our eyes begin to find every fault and every flaw on our external bodies. This habit turns swiftly into self-criticism and inevitably self-disgust.

From this learned, habitual place of disgust and criticism, learning to see our bodies through the eyes of love again is a process.

Do our children need to go through this process too?

Today, I find myself in suburban Brisbane, with two kids and a twenty-plus-year marriage. Family life is in many ways similar to my childhood. I wish I could tell you that I was bringing up my children in a Beauty Load-free wonderland, but alas, my children feel it and respond to it in their own ways. I have tried to minimise how much they feel the Load. One way I have very consciously attempted to do this is by healing my own pain and struggle around the way I look. For example, I have been very conscious not to go on diets or react to my own worry about my body or theirs. I have tried not to tell them they 'better not eat that in case you get chubby.' But over the years, I have struggled with the Beauty Load and they see it all. Also, the Beauty Load is much bigger than my influence on them: it is social and cultural, it is peer groups, fitting in and social media.

I worry about how much my kids perceive their value—positively or negatively—as having a direct relationship to the way they look. I wish looks had nothing to do with their perceived value. But then, I have definitely praised them for being cute, handsome and pretty. It is complicated.

The Beauty Load is not helped by the relatively new influence of social media. We are bombarded with images and curated impressions of idealised bodies without really knowing what is true and what is not. To make things harder, it is teen girls who are the ones most addicted and also most affected. I remember the comparison of teen years being hard enough, without being bombarded in this way.

Then introduce COVID-19 to disrupt our routines, make us feel anxious and have us turn to our phones for support. COVID has meant, for a lot of us, that we are on Zoom calls or FaceTime a lot more than usual. We are confronted with our own faces a whole lot more, exposing our perceived flaws and giving us more time to scrutinise, judge and get self-critical.

My work as a counsellor has helped normalise the pressure of the Beauty Load for me and helped me to see more clearly that this is something we all feel, regardless of how we look. Through my work, I have had the honour of gaining insight into the beliefs, worries and anxieties that we humans—and in particular, women—share. It is through my role as a counsellor that I have become passionate, angry, worried and hopeful about this reality and feel compelled to unpack it here with you.

I imagine that you, like me and my clients, have felt the Beauty Load from an early age. Probably from before you were a teenager. I mean, can you remember a time in your life in which the idea of being 'pretty enough' has *not* been an instinctual part of who you are and what you consider when you get ready to interact with the people around you? I can't.

The truth is that worrying about how we look takes up substantial space in our lives. We think about how we come across, worry that we are not quite enough, compare ourselves with others, criticise ourselves for any flaws, wish away the kilos and stare into the mirror looking for more.

So subtle. So pervasive. But what exactly is the Beauty Load and where does it come from? Let's explore that in the next chapter.

WHAT MAKES IT HARD FOR YOU TO ACCEPT YOUR LOOKS?

The following are comments from women in my network.

- 'I have put on some weight recently and my clothes are all tight. It's a daily reminder that I'm not at my ideal weight.'
- 'I was teased a lot going into high school for my face. I had bad skin and a bad haircut, just bad timing. It has truly scarred how I feel inside and out. I have felt embarrassed talking to people and taking photos of myself, and always feel very awkward wondering if people are struggling to look at my face.'
- 'I have larger teeth, more than average body hair, and small breasts.'
- 'Small breasts, extra weight around my middle. Not feeling feminine.'
- 'Wanting my body to look a certain way. I wish I had a flat stomach. This causes me a lot of distress.'
- 'The cellulite bumps on my bum and legs, [which are] now growing up my arms.'
- 'I hate where I put weight on. I feel very unfeminine. I look like a fat boy. I wish I had curves.'
- 'I'm bigger and chubbier than I want to be and I don't look like the pretty girls.'
- 'Feeling a bit chubby in clothes.'

Chapter 3

What is the Beauty Load?

When you're getting ready to go out, whether to the shops or to dinner, do you just grab the first thing you see in your wardrobe and chuck it on without thinking?

Most of the time, I'm guessing, probably not.

Instead, you'll probably consider, at least for a moment—sometimes for a lot longer than that—how you will look to others.

The level of concern you hold for this will vary depending on the event, your relationship to any other people involved, the day, your mood, even your time of the month.

There will be days when you don't give a shit what people think, and you grab the first thing you see. There will be other days where you just cannot decide what to wear, and even after you've tried on eleven outfits, nothing seems good enough and you don't feel pretty enough no matter what you look like.

Imagine this for a moment. You are at a party, and you have the realisation that you didn't quite 'nail' your outfit. You feel all wrong and conspicuous. It could be that you have had a wardrobe malfunction, or realised that your jeans are actually way too tight. It could be that everyone else seems to have the same uber-cool dress code and under the bright lights you see that what you threw together just doesn't work. I invite you to take a moment to tune in. How would you feel in this situation? Would you feel confident, energised and ready to mingle?

I am guessing not.

When this happens to me, I feel terrible. I don't just feel that I don't *look* good, but I start to feel bad about my whole self and sense of belonging. In those moments, it feels difficult to separate myself and my worth from the way I look. The outfit stuff-up seems to have the power to block access to my confidence, swallow it up whole and make me feel utterly unworthy. I could probably still mingle and meet people, but I would be less comfortable, more anxious. I wouldn't have the same sparkling energy about me as I would if I were feeling 'beautiful'.

The above example is just a mere outfit. My sense of unworthiness can be even worse if I have put on a few kilos over my 'happy weight', have a rash of pimples on my face or find myself thrust into a group of supermodel types. Gad!

I feel the Beauty Load like a heavy weight in moments such as these. It sits in my heart like embarrassment and gives me an icky discomfort that makes me want to run away and hide. It feels like shame, anxiety, or at worst, self-loathing. Is it just me, or do you feel this too?

The Beauty Load comes in many guises, which is why I describe it as a constant undercurrent of worry. Concerns stemming from the Beauty Load about being beautiful enough can include, but are not limited to, worrying about:

- Our shape and fitness
- Our weight
- Our make-up
- Our hair or hairstyle
- Our skin
- Our age or signs of aging

- Our clothes and style
- Our appropriateness
- How fashionable and 'on trend' we are
- What others think
- How much we belong
- How safe we are in a world where 'beauty' can make you a target
- How invisible we are in a world where not fitting the standards makes you disappear

PAUSE FOR A MOMENT AND REFLECT
What are the biggest beauty worries for you?

The Beauty Load weighs heavy in our hearts and on our shoulders, draining us of our joy, and making us stressed, exhausted and often resentful. It is felt in most cultures around the world. Different cultures will have different expectations, but within the dominant Western, consumerist, Christian-based culture that I am a part of, the expectations are overwhelming and unavoidable in mainstream, everyday life.

The Beauty Load makes us feel unhappy with ourselves and then keeps feeding that. It causes an endless cascade of negativity inside of us.

Some of the internal effects the Beauty Load has on us are:

- Insecurity
- Comparison
- A desire to change or fix ourselves
- A depletion of money, time and energy
- Negative self-talk
- Self-loathing

- Opting out of participating in things that we value
- A fear of being seen
- Feeling unworthy of love
- A disconnect from our pleasure

Overall, the Beauty Load makes women, in particular, feel like they are not good enough, not lovable enough … not enough.

The Beauty Load is not just a heavy weight in the way it feels; it also creates more for us to *do*. Have you heard of the term 'the mental load'? It is the invisible, never-ending mental work of maintaining a house and family that is very often left to the women. And then there is the emotional load. Another task often left to women, which is more invisible work, this time to do with maintaining relationships and managing emotions. The Beauty Load is yet another invisible load. We pile it on top of our weary shoulders, balancing it above the mental and emotional loads of managing our homes, careers, lives, families and relationships, but this time, we are stressed out about our appearance.

The stress and worry of the Beauty Load has us soldier on with these ever-expanding beauty to-dos:

- Shaving our legs
- Watching the scales
- Doing our nails
- Whitening our teeth
- Getting braces
- Waxing
- Putting together an outfit
- Going shopping
- Doing our hair
- Putting on make-up

- Choosing the right shoes
- Trying to avoid getting wrinkles, acne, blemishes and stretch marks
- Plucking
- Filing
- Moisturising
- Contouring
- Taking pills and potions to keep us looking 'young and smooth'
- Monitoring what we eat
- Dieting
- Keeping up with the trends
- Dying our hair
- Bleaching our skin (for some)
- Fake tanning our skin (for others)
- Threading
- Choosing the right accessories
- Finding the right jewellery
- Wearing contact lenses
- Getting piercings

More things to do and prepare that sap our time, money and energy.

Many of us don't even question it or notice how much space it's taking up, because these preparations have become part of the job that we just get on with and do. This is just normal, isn't it? Getting ready to go out, preening ourselves in the mirror, shopping for new clothes (because whoever has anything to wear?), feeling lacking; these are all things that we throw ourselves into as a kind of necessary 'hobby'. It has become part of the task of feeling 'good enough' in the world as a woman.

Do we enjoy it, though? So many women seem to make a hobby or look after themselves with activities such as shopping, tanning and getting their nails done. Is it really fun? Is it really self-care? Perhaps we don't enjoy the process so much as we enjoy the confidence or sense of safety and belonging that the pastimes bring us.

PAUSE FOR A MOMENT AND REFLECT

What are the beauty rituals that you spend most of your time on?

Do you enjoy these rituals? Or do you enjoy the confidence that the rituals bring? Or both?

These questions feel like a bit of a contradiction.

There are quite a few contradictions with the Beauty Load, so let's clear them up from the get-go.

1. DEEP DOWN, THERE'S A PART OF US THAT STILL FEELS BEAUTIFUL

Despite the stress, the worry, the self-critical thoughts and the lengths we are willing to go to for beauty, there is a more optimistic, loving part of ourselves that does see our inherent beauty. It is the part of us that we connect to when we get out into the wilderness and beyond the influence of the culture. The Self. The Self knows our beauty. It sees the kind of beauty that is based on being a good-enough human with a beating heart and life force coursing through you.

The Self gives us a deep knowing that our looks are enough just as they are and that there are many other valuable aspects to who we are. This knowing is deep and central to our true being.

It is there, immutable within us all. But often it is drowned out by our noisier, nigglier negative parts that tend to take over when we are down or lost amidst the societal pressure of the Beauty Load. Somehow, the negativity manages to erase all memory of this other, more loving part of ourselves, filling us with doubt, fear and the kneejerk response to fix ourselves. Sometimes the fear is all we can hear.

PAUSE FOR A MOMENT AND REFLECT
Do you feel this more optimistic, loving part of
yourself (however faintly)?
When was the last time you felt this loving part of you?

2. DESPITE THE WEIGHT OF THE LOAD, WE DON'T WANT TO STOP OUR QUEST FOR BEAUTY

Personally, even though carrying this heavy load on my shoulders has caused so much distress and insecurity, the idea of completely letting the quest for beauty go does not interest me, nor does it interest the women around me, when I have asked them. We love beautiful things. We love appreciating the way things look. Taking care of and receiving joy from aesthetics feels like an intrinsic and valuable part of being feminine (possibly even human) that we don't want to let go of. I want to maintain my beauty rituals, albeit with more beneficial intentions. I want them as a way of connecting with myself, rather than a way to continue to play into false beauty beliefs that come from a place of deficit.

Do you feel the Beauty Load has given you many positives?
Do you take pleasure from beauty rituals?
Would you be willing to give your quest for beauty up?

3. PRETTINESS IS NOT THE SAME AS BEAUTY

For the purposes of this book, I am talking about beauty both in the sense of beauty as a characteristic or quality and *prettiness*. Beauty is defined in the dictionary as 'the quality present in a thing or person that gives intense pleasure or deep satisfaction'.[1] It can be used in a similar way to 'pretty' without a doubt, but the difference seems to be that where *pretty* is just about being pleasing to the eye, *beauty* has a sense of giving pleasure and satisfaction to those who admire it. The capacity to give these feelings of pleasure must come from a deeper place than the surface, as it has the power to touch the heart and soul of those in its presence ... which makes me think that the advertising industry has us barking up the wrong tree. They are selling us pretty and we are aspiring to look good on the surface, but in essence, we want something deeper; we want to feel something. We want to offer pleasure and satisfaction to those around us; in essence, we want something beyond the surface. We want to *be* beautiful.

PAUSE FOR A MOMENT AND REFLECT
In your definition, what is the difference between
pretty and beautiful?
Which do you aspire to more —being pretty or beautiful?

4. WE ARE NOT SURE WHO WE ARE WANTING TO LOOK BEAUTIFUL FOR

When we are young and single, our sense of 'not enough' becomes entrenched in the idea that we need to look better in order to find a partner. For women with heterosexual tendencies, this becomes about looking good for men. We want male attention, we want them to find us alluring and attractive. This is akin to what feminist film theorist Laura Mulvey refers to as 'the male gaze'[2] in which the female body is sexualised and objectified in the media for male pleasure. With exposure to the male gaze over many years, we become programmed to such a degree that we start to see ourselves via the lens of the male gaze, becoming at once validated by it, and fearful of the attention and potential harassment that comes with it.

Later, when we find a partner and are settled in the relationship, we are surprised that the urge to look better is still with us. We still want the male gaze to validate us. But, if we are in a secure relationship, why should this matter? We feel it when we are in the company of women too. We wonder to ourselves, *Who am I even wanting to look good for?* Our brain has become wired to rely on our radar of how much we are noticed and desired to gauge our worth. Yet, often, the beauty standards and rituals that we set for ourselves are established and 'critiqued' not by men, but by other women.

PAUSE FOR A MOMENT AND REFLECT
Who do you want to look good for?

OUR LOOKS NEVER FEEL 'ENOUGH'

The Beauty Load is the cultural and societal pressure that makes us look at others in comparison and feel like we're not good enough. We judge our looks by the responses we get from strangers, our reflection in the mirror, or the selfie we take on our phone. The irony is, if we were truly striving for beauty, we would not be just looking at a snapshot of our looks on the surface. Instead, we would be thinking about the effect we have on all those around us; we would ponder whether it is an effect of 'intense pleasure or deep satisfaction'. If we did this, perhaps the Beauty Load would not be such a problem.

The Beauty Load is a problem, though, in that it has us wanting to look good, but leaves us feeling a lack of whatever is needed to fit the 'beauty' mould. From this sense of lack cascades feelings of insecurity, uncertainty about our value, and—crucially—the thinking we *need to do more* to feel good about ourselves.

Most women think about their looks, which is fine. What is not fine is that concerns about how we look negatively impact how we feel about ourselves. We put an outfit together and surely that is enough. But it's not! We fret over whether it looks right, goes together, suits us, fits in, is pretty enough/trendy enough, makes our butt look big, is age appropriate or too revealing or too prudish. And this fretting turns into doubting and, at worst, hating who we are. *Ach!*

Are you always wondering if you look good enough?

Do you feel the worry of needing to look a certain way so you can feel worthy?

Is the list of beauty to-dos consuming you?

Or perhaps you're even wondering if you have been spared the Beauty Load. The next chapter will help you work that out.

Chapter 4

But I'm not affected by this Beauty Load you speak of!

You may be reading this wondering what the big deal is about bodies and looks. 'Get over it!' you might say. If you are thinking that, I can only imagine you are either:

a) not a woman
b) not from the same dominant, Western, consumerist culture as I am
c) one of the small percentage of women blessed with an agreed-upon perfect bod (which is no guarantee of feeling great, by the way, as we'll explore later)
d) just blessed to be blissfully untroubled by it

But if you're reading this, my guess is that you get the Beauty Load on some level. Of course, it is a spectrum. On one end of the spectrum are those whose body image is as stable and comfortable as a five-star-resort bed. On the other end of the spectrum is a great deal of hard-cold-floor suffering.

You may not feel like you are that affected by the Beauty Load and that this obsession has happily skimmed you by.

But is this really true?

Perhaps it is, or maybe you are so immersed in the normality of the Beauty Load within our culture that you can't see it. One of the very problems with the Beauty Load is the way it permeates our unconscious.

If you were an alien arriving on this planet, into this culture, you would see the Beauty Load in all its complex, self-esteem-stealing glory. But we think it is normal. 'This is just the way life is,' we say. 'It's just the way humans are. It is totally natural … isn't it?'

Let's do a quick quiz to see if the Beauty Load has rested on your shoulders at all. See how many of the following 'Have you ever' questions you answer yes to.

HAVE YOU EVER:

Felt like you had nothing to wear?
It's odd really, isn't it? You have enough clothes, yet when a special occasion arises with the people you really want to impress, you feel like you have absolutely nothing to wear.

I'm in the privileged situation of having a wardrobe full of clothes (albeit mostly thrifted), yet I still get this feeling.

The last time I felt like this was about a week ago, when I was going out to dinner with some girlfriends. Nothing I tried on felt good enough. It took me four outfit changes to land on something that I was happy enough to wear to leave the house.

Felt that you couldn't be attractive or find love the way you were?
When I was younger, the story I told myself about myself was that I would never find a partner because of the way that I looked. Men, I decided, needed women to have breasts of a certain size to find them attractive, and that was not me.

I was certain that I was destined for a life of loneliness all because of my A-cup breasts.

For some, the fear of not being worthy of love due to the way they look can make them insecure, put up with shit they shouldn't, or even put love and romance in the too-hard basket.

Batted away compliments?

'You look stunning!' a friend told me. Even though I loved the compliment, I didn't feel like I could simply accept it; that would be a little too uncomfortable. Instead of a simple and gracious 'thank you so much', I replied, 'Oh, you must be saying that because you're not wearing your glasses!'

We not only repel compliments but will go out of our way to say negative things about the way we look, as though getting in there first saves us from the discomfort of someone saying something negative as a follow-up and surprising us with it. Does this work, though?

Been obsessed with your reflection?

This can go both ways. For some, we become obsessed with checking our looks on every reflective surface. *Is anything out of place? How do I look now?*

For others, we can become obsessed with not seeing our reflection—avoiding mirrors and reflective windows—to evade any reminders of how we look throughout the day. *I don't want to see it. I don't want to be reminded of my disappointment.*

Hated a certain body part?

There is that one part of your body that you just can't seem to forgive. It sticks out and taunts you every time you look in the mirror. Your focus seems to rest on it and its sins have multiplied in your eyes.

For me, it was always my breast size. For you, it might be your nose, belly, bum, skin, the list goes on ...

Avoided intimacy?

You are getting all the signs and signals that intimacy is there for the enjoying and you feel the thrill of anticipation deep in your loins, but no! You pull the plug and pull out, excusing yourself due to 'having to get up early in the morning' or some other lame excuse. Really, what might have happened is you felt the rise of inadequacy and shame about your body. A negative voice in your head told you that if you followed that thrill towards intimacy and got your clothes off and bared all, you would be bound for certain rejection. So ... best to pull out now and save yourself the hurt.

Avoided social engagements?

Many of my clients report that they avoid social engagements and outings because they are worried about how they look. The idea of going out and being around people who may judge them or be all 'perfectly put together' themselves just feels too daunting and hard.

Been distressed by signs of aging?

You are not getting any younger, but it seems like the models and culturally endorsed 'beauties' are. The people you see on TV, in the media and in movies do not show any signs of aging. But you do. Your wrinkles, grey hairs and less-than-perky muscles (and breasts) distress you, as you know they are not getting any 'better'.

Now, in my late-forties, I have days when all I see are the lines, the sagging skin and the signs that my youth is fading. It can be quite daunting. Aging, older women are not held up as beautiful or valued in our culture very often and, as a result, losing our youth feels like a loss of value and credibility, making aging something to fear.

Felt like you didn't belong because of the way you looked?
You feel fine about yourself at home, but when you are at a bar or the beach and everyone around you seems to have a great figure and perfect tan—or just seems to fit the beauty ideal a whole lot more than you—you seem to sink into a self-confidence black hole. Some of my non-white clients have reported that this happens to them. They would find themselves as the only one of a minority racial group in a room and all of a sudden feel awkward, unattractive and like they wanted to run and hide.

Sometimes, this shows itself as jealousy, a sudden wish for your partner to not be witness to that 'other' beauty, as a scared part of us fears that they might want to switch to the more beautiful model.

Leveraged the power of your beauty?
We can hate a system that diminishes our value to the placement, size and colour of external features, but we can also leverage the power that beauty gives us. Whether it be to push forward and get served at a busy bar, to play sweet and get away with things under an authority figure, or to get ahead, many of us have at some time or another used our beauty to get us the things we want or need.

Noticed that your friends feel less attractive than they are?
Have you noticed that you can see the Beauty Load more clearly in those around you? Your friends are beautiful, but you notice that they seem quite hung up and lacking in confidence around the way they look. You just don't understand their concern over seemingly small blemishes or issues.

'So what if you are a few kilos over your happy weight? Your curves are sexy. What's the big deal about your grey hair? It looks kind of regal.'

'Your nose is you and I love you.'

But your friends don't find it quite that easy to accept themselves and their confidence reflects this, to your great disappointment.

Noticed that you feel concerned about the appearance of your loved ones?

Have you noticed that you feel a pit of dread about the appearance of a certain close family member or friend when you are presenting them to others? It might be their overt sexiness, lack of cleanliness or care, disregard for the rules of the social group you are presenting them to, or the idea that they have "let themselves go". Whatever it is, in these moments, it feels like the judgement for them will be directed at you through association. You may find yourself making comments to "help" your loved one present better, but really the hope is that you will feel less judged.

How did you go? So, have you ever felt the pressure of the Beauty Load?

I imagine you have been touched by the effects of one or all of these experiences. Many of us are not just touched lightly as a one-off, but feel the ongoing beauty pressure bearing down on us: cold, hard and constant.

If you answered yes to any of these scenarios, I am sorry to say that means you have indeed been burdened to some extent by the Beauty Load. You have felt a weight, possibly struggled with your self-worth and been battered by its toxic inner influence.

One thing that perhaps makes the burden easier to bear is that you are not carrying this load alone. Millions of women afflicted would, if they were reading this book, be nodding along with you. I would go as far as to say that the Beauty Load is inevitable for a woman, or any human, living in a Western culture in the world today. It is nothing to be ashamed of; in fact, it is completely normal, if you too carry the Load.

Chapter 5

I am not like Elle Macpherson

I was a different kind of beautiful to what I wanted to be.

Especially as a teenager, I wanted to be the kind of beautiful that was paraded in front of me day after day in the media. I wanted to look like Elle Macpherson, Cindy Crawford or Claudia Schiffer; the women I had plastered all over my high school exercise books.

The Beauty Load made me believe that in order to feel confident and comfortable in my body, I needed to meet a preordained ideal of beauty, something akin to perfection. Something like what those supermodels had.

The preordained idea of 'perfect' beauty that I aspired to as a teen was:

- being tall and slim with a neat figure (no cellulite, love handles, rolls, flab or excess fat)
- having smooth, blemish-free, white skin with a tan (certainly no freckles, at least not as many as I had!)
- having large blue or green, clear eyes
- having lustrous, thick, long blonde or brown hair
- having a small nose and symmetrical face
- having pert, C-cup breasts
- not having too much hair on the arms or legs, or, of course, the underarms

- being young
- being able bodied
- being feminine; looking and dressing like a woman

As if that wasn't hard enough to achieve, apparently these days it is even harder. The current-day desired figure is muscly and toned, yet with a curvy bust and bum; a difficult if not impossible look to achieve, because most commonly once you get the rippling muscles, you lose the curves.

Back in my day, I ticked a few of the features on the above list, but it was, as you perhaps felt yourself, not enough. I was different to the ideal and that made me feel uncomfortable about myself and my body.

If I didn't look like them, and they were the epitome of 'beauty', then the obvious conclusion I drew was that I must not be beautiful and needed to do more, be more and buy more in order to be okay. I was already looking for a reaction from the male gaze. I was very much already primed to become one of the masses spending billions trying to feel better about the way I looked.

PAUSE FOR A MOMENT AND REFLECT
Who were your beauty idols?
What was the beauty ideal you aspired to as a teen?

FITTING IN

The reason I felt this strong urge to be more or different was that I wanted to fit in. More than anything else, the Beauty Load is about fitting in. For our safety-conscious nervous system, fitting in, at its roots, means survival. This makes a lot more sense for our savanna-living, predator-avoiding ancestors than it does for us, as for them, not fitting in with the clan would mean being an isolated individual in a dangerous, sabre-tooth world; in other words, it would mean certain death. The wiring in our brains has not changed much since then, despite our surroundings changing a lot. We still feel the heightened reactions—the sense of doom and panic that our nervous system plummets into when there is the merest whiff of rejection. We are, after all, creatures who survive best by staying with the tribe, and this means fitting in.

When we are focussed on fitting in, our protective parts take over, which we will talk more about in Chapter 9. For now, what's important is that our primal drive to fit in makes us vigilantly focus on the world and the people around us.

Which doesn't sound that bad, does it? I mean, we just want to fit in with those around us. We just want to be 'normal', so we notice what everyone else is doing and we avoid sticking out like a sore thumb. We want to sit with the majority of other 'normal' humans on the bell curve of average.

So, why then do we aspire to be like the supermodels? The average human, in the middle of the bell curve, is not like them. If we just want to be 'normal', surely what most of us see when we look in the mirror would be enough.

Dolly Alderton sums it up in this quote from her 2020 book *Everything I Know about Love*: 'To be a desirable woman—the sky's the limit. Have every surface of your body waxed. Have manicures every week. Wear heels every day. Look like a Victoria's Secret Angel even though you work in an office. It's not enough to be an average-sized woman with a bit of hair and an all-right jumper. That doesn't cut it. We're told we have to look like the women who are paid to look like that as their profession.'

AVERAGE IS NO LONGER ENOUGH

The Beauty Load has shifted the goalposts. Our goal has moved from finding safety and self-acceptance through fitting into the norm of the people around us, to wanting to sit at the perfect end of the bell curve informed by the models and celebrities. This tendency in humans to compare ourselves with those who we perceive to be 'better' than us is known as upward comparison.[3] Upward and downward comparison are normal human behaviours that help us both gauge how we are doing and where we are, but also set a benchmark for what we aim to achieve.

Is it possible that our exposure to so many images of perfection in the media has warped our natural default awareness of what normal looks like?

Our communities used to be small. For most of human history, our influence was as wide as our tribe or our village was big. But now, with TV, Instagram, Snapchat, TikTok and the rest, we are comparing ourselves with photoshopped, filtered and collated versions of an enormous community, the whole world. It is like beauty is a hierarchy and the higher we rise, the more safety we have in our culture … which makes sense, but it is not normal to be comparing ourselves with these images of 'perfection'. Do we really need to be 'perfect' to feel good enough?

A 2019 blog post by Australian media figure Mia Freedman sums this up perfectly.[4] Freedman was starting to notice that her eyelashes were thinner and maybe shorter too. She was aware that whenever she noticed her short, thin eyelashes, she felt bad about them, but just dismissed it as another one of those things that happens to us when we age. Then she realised what had happened: 'Now that eyelash extensions have become mainstream and I'm seeing them on women I know and women on Instagram, on newsreaders and celebrities (and obviously on Kardashians), my eyes have adjusted and what used to look a bit drag-queeny and overdone has become the new baseline in my subconscious for what eyelashes *should* look like.' Our minds get so used to seeing the images that they become our new normal and our new desirable, to the point that not embodying this need makes us feel bad about ourselves. The trends are constantly changing; no matter what lashes we extend, bangs we get cut or fake tan we apply, things will change. There will always be more.

Whatever is going on, the Beauty Load is not good for our body image or the health of our relationships with our bodies. Statistics from the National Eating Disorders Collaboration (2012) show that seventy per cent of adolescent girls in Australia are not satisfied with their bodies,[5] with body image being identified as one of the top three ranked issues of personal concern for young people in the 2010 Mission Australia Youth Survey.[6]

IT'S NOT JUST ADOLESCENTS

A 2016 study published in the *Australian and New Zealand Journal of Public Health* reported that eighty per cent of female participants experienced some level of body dissatisfaction.[7] It seems that normal and healthy is just not enough for us. The goal is to sit at the perfect end of the bell curve and nowhere else, even when we are healthy adults.

YET WE ALL KNOW THAT NO BODY IS PERFECT

The beauty ideal that we see plastered all over the media is a mirage. It is created with airbrushing, lighting, filters and make-up. It isn't real and we know it isn't real. Yet, what do we do? Instead of remembering that it is all a fake impossibility, we think to ourselves, *Well, I don't look like that. I look different, so I will cover up or change this body of mine and try to be more like them.* We set our minds to it and can sometimes become crazed in our pursuit.

Let's focus in on the pressure to be skinny for a moment.

The models, actresses and stars that we aspire to look like—whose images are helping create this new idea of 'normal'—will often starve themselves in order to achieve the beauty ideal.[8] A study in Hungary shows that the use of diuretics and appetite suppressants are more prevalent in models than the general population, as are eating disorders.[9] Victoria's Secret models are a case in point. At its peak, the Victoria's Secret runway show was watched by more than 33 million viewers live. Being cast as a Victoria's Secret model could make or break a model's career, yet the twenty or so models who are 'picked' have a gruelling diet and fitness regime in the months leading up to the show, to the point of dehydration, illness and collapse.[10] Does that sound like fun? Is this what we are aspiring to?

We are seeing skinny models, actresses and stars who are a long way under the average weight and yet this is normalised and the Beauty Load has us aim for it as if it were the bell-curve-normal that we ought to aspire to. Skinny, after the endless amount of imagery we have been exposed to, has become not only desirable, but our 'normal'. This has been helped along by the medicalisation of weight. Nineteenth-century doctors equated plumpness to good health.[11] But by the 1920s, with an increase in overabundance and over-consumption, things shifted and fat became a metaphor for excess and cause for shame, and within the medical realms, 'overweight' moved from being a sign or symptom to being a disease.[12] Now our doctors monitor our weight, adding health as a factor for 'fitting in' while too-skinny models are collapsing, losing their menstrual cycles and needing to exist on drips between shoots. Go figure?

Getting skinny may be a sure-fire way to be on trend in the beauty stakes, but statistics show that it doesn't make us happy. Skinniness correlates directly with body dissatisfaction and low self-esteem.[15]

Skinny, to the degree that is desirable, while fashionable, is not happy and neither is it healthy (unless it is our natural state). The female figure needs some fat to be healthy.[16] The casualties of dieting and controlled eating are not just our sanity but also our menstrual cycle and libido, and the health of our skin, hair and nails. Not to mention the loss of pleasure from the sensual act of enjoying food.

A friend of mine recently commented that she is the heaviest she has ever been in her life, which makes her feel uncomfortable and unattractive. But it's not all bad, she also noted that she has also never been so happy, like there is joy bubbling up from within that has never been there before and her libido has never been so strong.

Skinny does not necessarily make us feel good, and it can steal the joy of our bodies, senses, cycles, food and sexuality.

Does being skinny or slim really equate to beauty? It's certainly not always healthy. In Chapter 23, we look at health as a key marker in attraction.

PAUSE FOR A MOMENT AND REFLECT
What is your relationship with slimness?

Chapter 6

Feeling sexy in Cuba

If you'd asked me or any of my friends as teens if we thought we were beautiful, we would have replied with an adamant 'No!' and swiftly filled you in on all the problem areas of our bodies—blemishes here, pockets of cellulite there, excessive hair in places we would rather it wasn't, marks, pimples, you name it. Sadly, we would probably still say the same things thirty-plus years later … this is the Beauty Load.

I presumed this was normal, just the life of a woman until, a few years ago, I stumbled upon a fabulous TV series called *The Sunny Side of Sex* by Dutch presenter Sunny Bergman. In her quest to explore sex in different cultures around the world, Bergman took her queries to Cuba. There was one scene in which she visited a gym and caught a bunch of women on their way out of an exercise class. Bergman gathered the women around and asked them some questions. The first was: Do you think you're sexy?

I knew what the answer would be if this same scene were playing out in any gym in modern-day Australia. It would be a lot like my schoolmates back in the eighties. 'Sexy? Hell no!' followed up immediately by the evidence of their flaws and inadequacies.

But the Cuban women's answers—and gestures—left me shocked and started the explorations that would lead me to write this book.

These women were all shapes and sizes. They were curvy, buxom, skinny and flat, light-skinned, dark-skinned and everything in between. Yet, all of them, when asked this question, rather than delivering an instantaneous denial from their heads, dropped into their bodies and started moving. The question initiated a sensual response. As they answered, you could see them sway, touch their bodies and basically start gyrating as they said, 'Sexy? Of course I'm sexy!' And those Cuban women were indeed sexy, inside and out.

When asked why they thought they were sexy, they looked quizzically at the presenter as if to say *What do you mean?* before proudly stating 'Because I am a woman.'

It was as simple as that. They were beautiful and sexy because they were women. Being a woman was enough in and of itself.

Over the years, as I loosen my mind's grip on the mantra that I am unattractive, I realise (like really realise) that beauty is not about the view from outside. It is an attitude and feeling that radiates from within. It is an ownership of who we are, creating an effect on those around us.

The Cuban women did not resemble what I'd been told the sexy or beauty ideal was, but the minute they connected in with their bodies and their beliefs about themselves, their beauty was radiant, authentic and obvious.

I was chatting over coffee with a friend recently, and she let it slip that she had lived in Cuba for a year in her twenties.

'How was it?' I enquired, telling her that I had heard women felt beautiful there.

'I have never felt so happy or more beautiful in my life,' she said, before going on to confirm that it didn't seem to matter how you presented yourself; if you were a woman, that was enough to be considered beautiful.

What is the difference then between me and my friends, and these Cuban women? Where did they get their internal permission? How did they see and connect with their inner radiance, while I just missed mine completely?

I have never been to Cuba, but from what I understand from my reading and research, the answer is related to both culture and exposure. Cuban culture, while it surely has its gender issues, reveres the feminine as beautiful. The fact that you are a woman in Cuba seems to be enough to claim your beauty.

I do not want to suggest that there is no Beauty Load in Cuba; I am sure there is still the pull to fit in and to rise on the hierarchy of acceptability. But from what I can see, the Beauty Load feels different there.

But perhaps there is more. Possibly related to this is the lack of advertising in Cuba. These women are not sold 'beautiful bodies'. For half a century after the revolution in 1959, advertising was limited in Cuba to patriotic propaganda.[16] The Cubans, particularly the women, have not been subjected to millions of images of what is a good, right or beautiful way to look. They are not constantly in a state of comparison to some idealised beauty 'norm'.

It is hard to know how many ads we are exposed to on a daily basis in the Western world, but approximations state that we see six thousand and potentially up to ten thousand ads a day per person[14]—a figure that has doubled since 2007 and I imagine will only keep on rising.

Does seeing ads really affect us? The Cuban example does not stand alone. Case in point: a study done by Harvard Medical School anthropology professor Anne Becker on young girls in Fiji. In Fijian culture, 'You've put on weight' was not traditionally the comment to strike dread into a young woman's heart. It was a compliment. Curves and a more robust figure were admired.

And then came the introduction of the TV and with it our westernised cultural ideals and skinny superstars.

Becker was an anthropologist on the ground, noting the difference in the young women before and after TV (and with it, advertising) was introduced. What she found clearly shows that our insanity around beauty, skinniness and body dissatisfaction is linked to the media. Within three years of TV, there was a sudden increase in eating disorders, and where previously girls had been satisfied with their bodies, now they were making comments while watching TV such as 'I want their body' and 'I want their size.' And over eleven per cent of the girls studied reported that they had purged to lose weight at least once. By 2007, this figure was up to forty-five per cent.

PAUSE FOR A MOMENT AND REFLECT
Does having a break from exposure to ads make a
difference to how you feel about yourself?

When I see an advertisement, I don't think I'm taking it in or that it is affecting me. I feel like I'm stronger than the subliminal messaging or the meaning inside the images I'm seeing, and I certainly do not want to let some advertisement manipulate my mind and tell me what I want to think, least of all about myself. But alas, it seems that in my early adult years (and no doubt now too) the ads got to me, as they get to all of us. In my physical prime, with my body as youthful, supple and radiant as it would ever be, I felt inadequate. I felt an utter incompleteness that stole my ability to claim my beauty, my sexiness or my confidence.

Chapter 7

Beauty, love and marriage through time

Was the Beauty Load a heavy burden before advertising was a thing?

Cleopatra was said to be a great beauty. Interestingly, actual records are reduced to an unappealing silhouette of her on a coin.[17] Was it her great beauty that won her the affections of both Julius Caesar and Mark Antony, as the modern narrative wishes to portray it?

Beauty has been something to aspire to for millennia, especially if you are a woman.

Our ideas of beauty have changed. In prehistory, the revered feminine fertility figure of the *Venus of Willendorf* shows a curvy, voluptuous body. In ancient Greece, said to be the birthplace of modern beauty ideals, the aim was symmetry and curvy female figures.[18] We have all seen the *Venus de Milo* and Rubens and Rembrandt paintings with their plump and curvy female forms, all in stark contrast to the 'skinny' beauty ideals of today.

In the seventeenth century, the plump female form was desired as a sign of wealth; a social status reserved for those who could afford the richer, fattier food and more sedentary lifestyle of the wealthy. In these eras, the hairline was desired to be high, and the skin pale, again as a sign of class, as it showed that you didn't have to go out in the fields to work.

At the onset of the Industrial Revolution, it became desirable for men to promote their own social status by having a thin, weak wife[19]—a wife who anyone could quite plainly see would not be able to do any manual labour or she would likely pass out. Thus, the thin ideal was born. Let's just repeat that, *our insanity around needing to be skinny was born from men wanting to flaunt their wealth and privilege.* When we say it like that, do we really want to be involved?

In the USA, just before the civil war around the mid-1800s, the fashion was for women to be so thin and pale so as to emulate someone with tuberculosis, thus showing their subservience to their man and their commitment to the domestic realm.[20] Again, not something most modern women would want to aspire to.

The working classes haven't had the privilege of being too ill to work. The traits that mattered to the working classes were, and still are, strength, health and fertility, from which a lot of our beauty ideals stem. The features that we generally agree across cultures as being keys to beauty are clear eyes; symmetry; red lips; the proportions between hips, waist and bust; and rosy cheeks—all signs of a healthy, fertile individual … which meant a productive, stable and practical marriage match.

It is interesting how these health markers have morphed and changed across cultures depending on sociopolitical factors:

- In Mauritania, the general beauty consensus is for a woman to have a more voluptuous figure with curves that would make a modern, Beauty Load-influenced woman want to have liposuction. In Mauritania, skinny means starving, while chubby means you can afford to eat well and historically was a sign of wealth (and still is in many parts).[21]

- In Western countries, having sun-kissed skin these days is highly sought after as a sign of health and wealth ('Who had a nice holiday on the Med?'), whereas, before the Industrial Revolution, the fashion was to have pale skin.[22]
- In many parts of Asia, having a tan is a sign that you had to spend your days working in a field. There, pale white skin is a sign of being of a higher class and is deemed beautiful, and therefore sought after.[23]

While wealth, health, strength and fertility were what mattered more for most of history, the Beauty Load intensified when marriage became more about love than productivity on the land or family strategy. Relationship expert Esther Perel reminds us that love marriages are a fairly new concoction, being only about sixty years old.[24] 'Not so long ago, the desire to feel passionate about one's husband would have been considered a contradiction in terms. Historically, these two realms of life were organised separately—marriage on one side and passion most likely somewhere else, if anywhere at all,' Perel says. Prior to that, regardless of class and status, marriage was very much a strategic transaction. Qualities that were sought after in a good match would have been: being a good worker; having specific, desirable skills; status; wealth; getting on with the in-laws; fertility; health; good genes; strength and endurance. And, let's face it, individuals mostly wouldn't have chosen their mate themselves; parents would have done that job for them.

The idea of choosing a mate for love would have been thought of as risky. As Perel suggests, love and desire were mostly found outside of the marriage, and, *sorry ladies*, mostly by men in the form of lovers. The risk of getting pregnant made sexual dalliances for women much more limited. If the idea of choosing a marriage partner for love was risky though, I can only imagine that the idea of choosing for looks was even more laughable … looks as a sign of health and fertility and good genes, sure, but that would be as far as it went.

It is only in recent decades that attraction has become an important quality in our mate selection. Ask anyone and they will tell you that finding their mate attractive is vital for the health and longevity of their relationship. But how important is it, really?

The Beauty Load has skewed our perception of physical attraction into being more vital than it needs to be. Other qualities—such as life values, personality, direction, compatibility, attachment styles and so on—are surely due a larger portion of the attraction pie.

Another historical influence on the way women feel about their looks originated with the *male-breadwinner family* idea, which rose to the heady status of 'normal' in the West in around the 1950s. The woman's role as a housewife tended to go hand in hand with looking good. The male-breadwinner model of marriage,[25] which we think of as a historical norm, was never a plausible or possible marriage model for most people prior to this generation due to the necessity of having both partners contributing to the workload, and nor is it, as most of us can testify to, an arrangement that works. But it still has influence over the way women feel about beauty.

Circa the 1950s, women were told to look their best, to have their hair done in curls when their husband got home from work and to then hand their husband his beer and slippers. Beauty mattered in marriage a great deal, especially if you were female. The advice was to look pretty but 'don't bother your husband with petty troubles and complaints when he comes home from work.'[26] Then there was this advice for when your husband got home from work from a 1950s home economics book (yep, this stuff was actually taught in schools): 'Touch up your make-up, put a ribbon in your hair, and be fresh looking.'

PAUSE FOR A MOMENT AND REFLECT
Do you remember your parents or grandparents
reflecting this 1950s attitude towards
women and beauty?

Lots has changed since then, but in other ways, the influence is not that far removed today. The 1950s was the era in which my parents' generation grew up. The messages that trickled through to me as the next generation echoed the idea that looking pretty was important for me as a girl and a woman.

Chapter 8

It affects us all

Unless you live completely off the grid or perhaps in a place like Cuba, there is no escaping the Beauty Load. It is like a thick smog in the atmosphere around us that is very hard to avoid breathing in. It will influence us all in different ways, with varying degrees of intensity, but here's the thing: nobody escapes it!

Thus far, I have talked about the Beauty Load as though it is limited to women, but nah!

MEN FEEL IT TOO

You might have a male partner who seems to nonchalantly chuck on the first thing he sees in his wardrobe. It might seem like there is no Load for him, and if he's lucky, you might be right. At least, it might not be too heavy a burden for him to carry.

However, consider the male stereotype of 'tall, dark and handsome'. Have you ever wondered how the short, pale men feel? They are told from an early age that the way they look is not sought after by the ladies. This, without a doubt, can cause insecurity and angst for those who don't fit the 'look'.

'Short-man syndrome' is a case in point; this is a desire found in some shorter men to inflate their abilities, personality or success in order to compensate for their culturally sought-after 'lack in height'.

Another sensitive spot for men is the top of their heads. My husband went bald before he was twenty. It was tough for him. Balding can be a real crisis for men; you can tell by the lengths they go to cover it up—toupees, comb-overs, hair replanting and constant cap wearing. You can also tell by the amount of advertising directed at men's scalps.

It can be hard when men, just like women, stick out of the bell curve of normal. Too short, too dark, too tall, too fat, too skinny, too hairy, not hairy enough, too pimply, too sweaty, too different. It can, just as for women, mess with their confidence and make them self-conscious.

Young men these days feel the Beauty Load more than ever. A large-scale study in the US showed that male body dissatisfaction rose from fifteen per cent in 1982 to forty-five per cent in 2012, with most young men wishing to be larger and more muscular.[27] At the extreme end of the malaise, men were at risk of muscle dysmorphic disorder, steroid use and eating disorders. The male beauty market is a growth industry, set to be worth more than $72 billion a year worldwide by the end of 2022. So yeah, it's tougher for men to feel good and confident in their bodies now more than ever.

The Beauty Load can certainly cause a lack of confidence that impacts men's participation and input in life. Through my work, however, I have observed a disparity between the way the sexes feel the Beauty Load. I do not want to diminish anybody's struggle with the Load, as there are many causal factors and influences. But here's what I've concluded: in general, there is not the same direct connection between the way men look and the way they feel about themselves—i.e. their confidence and self-esteem—as there is for women. Like anything, there are exceptions, but I have seen this pattern again and again in my work as a counsellor. Yumi Stynes described this in one of her *Ladies, We Need to Talk* podcast episodes (highly recommended) as the *gender beauty gap*.[28]

An example of the gender beauty gap is the beauty product market, which is worth approximately $500 billion a year, and of which women account for between eighty and ninety per cent of the spending.[29] Women are spending more and earning less, as the gender beauty gap snaps at the heels of the gender pay gap. In Australia, women earn on average $261.50 less than men each week.[30] We spend more on beauty and we earn less.

We all feel the Beauty Load, but women feel it more. So, what's going on?

When you think about it, the culture, history and expectations are different for men and women. Let's take a closer look at a few key reasons why the Beauty Load is generally different and often less extreme for men.

1. Women are encouraged to wear make-up to cover up their face as part of society's beauty standards, whereas men are not encouraged or expected to do this. The message that you could interpret from this—and that becomes a natural response to habitual covering up, whether consciously or subconsciously—is that men's faces are acceptable just the way they are, whereas women's need work to be shown/acceptable in public.

2. Women's bodies are objectified for the male gaze. We are taught to enjoy looking at a certain type of body (female) and to gain pleasure from it. We are taught to want to find validation in another's pleasure. This has been termed 'the male gaze'.

3. Girls tend to be treated differently to boys from an early age. They are traditionally told they are pretty, given bows and flowers to put in their hair, and then rewarded with attention for their beauty. Mostly, boys are not. They have other pressures, such as being told to be tough, strong and independent, but not much importance is put on the way they look. In general, women have been conditioned from an early age to believe that beauty gains validity, while men have not.

4. We have been raised in a patriarchy. Historically, women's voices and presence in society have not been valued. In the majority of cultures, men have been the dominant gender for millennia. They have been the ones making the deals, waging wars, building societies, and using their intelligence, creativity, prowess and strength to make advancements and create new worlds. Women, on the other hand, have been less able to take part in important conversations, if at all.

    One example of this is our right to have a say in a democratic vote, which across the world has only been granted in the last century, though it was relatively early here in Australia in 1903. Women have not had voices, nor been appreciated for their wisdom or ideas. Women's input has historically been stifled, so we have not been able to find our value, worth or power through our intellectual offerings; it has been our looks and our service to others that have given us our value.

5. Before the last few decades, for millennia women did not have personal sovereignty or freedom ... and in many places across the globe, still don't. A woman was,

until very recently, by law seen as a possession to be passed from her father to her new husband (referred to as coverture). This can be seen to this day in the traditional marriage ritual of the father 'giving away' his daughter.

The law of coverture (active until the mid-1800s) meant that when a woman married, she became, by law, a part of the property of her husband. As property, she had no rights and was completely dependent on the goodwill of her husband. A woman's power was in her marriageability, with this power swiftly handed over to her husband upon marriage. Her power was not her independence or input into society, so she was forced to find it elsewhere. I imagine that looking pretty, cute, sexy or nice might have been some of the most potent ways a woman could find power.

6. Girls are socialised to be kind and nice. Author, researcher and all-round legend Brené Brown said in an interview I was listening to recently 'Girls lose access to their voices, boys lose access to their hearts.'[31] Boom! We are raised in a patriarchy that has resulted in the pendulum swinging too far towards the masculine ideals of power, authority and ownership. These influences do not serve anyone. Losing access to the heart means losing access to connection to the world, to self and in intimate relationships, which is not great for our men, but this is not the topic of this book. For women, our voice has got lost in our need to be pleasant and supportive and not cause problems for others. Without our voice, what have we got? Our bodies. And

without a voice, we feel the pressure for our bodies to be pleasing on the eye and not cause disruption or offence to those around us. If we had a voice, if we felt like it was safe to take up space and make noise, would we feel we have to be so pleasing on the eye?

EVEN THE DALAI LAMA

Whilst Buddhism is the birthplace of transformational and empowering messages such as needing to find peace within, I have known for a long while that it is not really feminist friendly. Even still, my heart hurt when I heard the following about the Dalai Lama. The fourteenth Dalai Lama has always seemed like a beacon of heart-centred hope to me, in a world that seems so cut off from the heart. But alas, in 2010, when asked if his chosen replacement could be a woman, he went and said that she would need to be attractive: '... if she is an ugly female, she won't be very effective, will she?'[32] Just, no!

The differences between the experience of men and women have infiltrated our psyches. They have influenced the way we seek safety, see power and find acceptability in the world. The need for these pursuits has become more acute over the years for women than it has for men. Is it any wonder as women that our bodies, our beauty, have become a way for us to get more of what we need (safety and acceptance)? Is it any wonder that it feels important to us to feel beautiful to the depths of our bones?

Perhaps the Beauty Load being different for women than it is for men is best summed up by the experiences of Australia's first female prime minister, Julia Gillard. Australian heads of state had, prior to Julia, never been judged by their looks, but in her short three-year term, Julia received multiple negative comments and attacks about her appearance, such as: 'On what should have been one of the proudest days of Gillard's political career, she bungled it with a less-than-flattering haircut and a frumpy 80s tapestry print jacket ... Get yourself a stylist your own age.'[33] The fact that she got comments like this from women is perhaps a sign of the expectations women hold of each other too when it comes to the Load.

PAUSE FOR A MOMENT AND REFLECT

How did gender influence the Beauty Load differently
for you and your peers growing up?
How do you think the Beauty Load is different for
men and women?

When we ask the questions of the Beauty Load and gender, we must also ponder how it is for transgender and queer people. How does the Beauty Load feel for those who do not fit the cisgender norms? The Beauty Load asks us to conform to certain ideals of male and female in order to be accepted. While it is harder for many women than it is for men, at least as women we know the territory, but that territory is binary, not allowing much room for non-binary people. The pressure to fit in, can steal our liberation and self-expression at the best of times, but especially if you are queer.

BUT THE BEAUTY LOAD IS NOT JUST A GENDER ISSUE

The Beauty Load is a racial, class, ability, poverty and size issue. It is intersectional, in that the Load feels heavier the more of the aforementioned departures from the beauty ideal you inhabit. It is generally felt more by anyone who is not bang in the middle or at the top end of the bell curve of 'cultural norms' on all fronts.

And the bell curve of normal (or at least the perceived one in our minds, which is manipulated by advertising and the media) is not all that inclusive. Beauty—for women, it seems—is white, tall and cis female.

This means that in predominately white Western cultures, Middle Eastern, African, Asian, mixed, Aboriginal and other racial groups are likely to experience the Beauty Load more as they have been left out of the default 'look'. The beauty work of straightening the hair and cosmetic procedures to get double eyelids and paler skin allude to the pressure to fit that default Western 'white woman' look. While white people (in mainstream Western cultures) feel the Beauty Load as a pressure to measure up to the imagery of beauty that is just out of reach, for all other racial groups, the bell curve of normal barely even includes them.[34] It is not a problem of constant comparison so much as a problem of not being included much at all.

Tahnee Jash, an Aboriginal Indigenous/Fijian-Indian journalist, shared some thoughts about the Beauty Load and what that's been like growing up as a woman of colour in Australia: 'Reflecting back on my younger years, I realised a lot of my insecurities came from the society we live in. I never fit Australia's beauty ideals of a 'white eurocentric' poster girl that I saw in magazines I read, which was teaching me to focus on my 'flaws' rather than love and embrace who I am. Things that were simple for some of my peers, like styling hair or buying foundation has always been a struggle for me. When there were beauty products created for women of colour, words like "tame unruly hair" or "skin whitening" would be used to promote them, reinforcing that feeling of "other" or "less than".'

It is hard to feel like we fit in until we are seeing ourselves depicted and reflected in what we see around us. I will talk about the importance of having role models in Chapter 21 for this reason. Seeing ourselves represented normalises and validates who we are. We think, *They are just like me—alright, I must be okay*. Without the visual evidence that the way you are is 'normal', the struggle with the Beauty Load is harder and the load feels heavier.

When it comes to models, magazines and runways, there is still a long way to go. According to a 2016 study, 78.2% of all the models featured in the spring season's fashion adverts across the Western world were white. [35] In a breakdown of the statistics, 8.3% of models featured were black, 4% were Asian and 3.8% were Hispanic. This is an improvement in representation compared with the statistics from the year before, and things are improving, but considering the prediction that non-whites will make up a majority of the population in Europe and the USA by 2050, it is not reflective of the world's population and diversity, let alone those of these particular Western countries to which the study related.[36]

As the Beauty Load is at its root a desire to fit in and belong, it is felt more strongly the more we feel excluded from the depiction of acceptable and desirable. The less we recognise ourselves in the cultural narrative of beauty, the more we will struggle with our sense of self.

Gender is one factor but, as with many systemic issues, the Beauty Load is intersectional. It affects us women because we had no voices and no power. Its effect varies depending on how closely one 'fits into' the dominant white-male-power dynamic. It varies depending on whiteness and race, body ability or disability, gender, and sexual orientation.

PAUSE FOR A MOMENT AND REFLECT

Where did your personal Beauty Load
pressure come from?

THE 'BEAUTIFUL ONES' FEEL IT TOO

It is easy to presume that the Beauty Load is less heavy for the ones that happen to have the agreed-upon beauty markers, but the Load still weighs on them too.

I am sure you know of some conventionally beautiful women who seem to carry the Load heavily. A friend of mine growing up was typically 'beautiful'. One day, when her family were leaving the house for an outing, my friend was holding them up.

'Just hurry up!' the family cried, but my friend was in a state of panic.

'*I can't get my outfit right,*' she stressed.

'Don't worry about it, just come!' the family implored, perplexed and impatient.

But she just couldn't, and instead, fell in a heap of distress on the floor, going on to explain to them how hard it was to be 'the beautiful one': 'Everyone will look at me, expecting me to look pretty, and if I am not, it will just be humiliating.'

My colleagues and I see this in our therapy rooms too. It is the client that is stunning *in all the agreed-upon ways* who is often struggling the hardest. In sessions, it may be revealed that their past was filled with abuse, neglect or abandonment and that, because of this, one of their greatest struggles is their personal 'beauty'. The problem is often not that these women doubt that they are beautiful, but that for so long their sense of safety and wellbeing has been attached to meeting such a high standard of beauty that the pressure to maintain it is exhausting. Fashion, make-up, hair, figure, brows, nails, tan perfection. This is the only way some people have been appreciated and valued by others in a chaotic or unsafe world. The thought of letting the standard drop is terrifying, even if they're only popping out of the house for a loaf of bread.

For others, beauty has been the reason they were targeted or abused. Covering up, hiding their figures, putting on weight; hiding their beauty can be a way to find safety.

I always thought that life seemed sweeter for the 'beautiful' ones. They seemed to get the friends, get the boyfriends, get the jobs. Beauty seemed like a passport to success. There is a definite 'hierarchy' of beauty with tangible benefits, and most of us just wish so badly that we could claim the passport to beauty success and live it large.

Is beauty a passport? In many ways it is. Studies have shown that beauty does gain benefits. In the workplace alone, research shows that physically attractive individuals are more likely to get the interview, advance faster in their careers and earn more money. Other studies have shown that the beauty 'halo' effect, a tendency for positive impressions to affect our judgement of people, sees beauty gaining people better grades at school, more friends and sexual partners and even less harsh penalties in the justice system.[37]

But the thing with the Beauty Load is that there is no free ride; wherever we sit on the bell curve has its burden. With the ever-present 'tall-poppy syndrome effect', especially here in Australia, a woman being too beautiful could mean she is not hired, thought more intimidating, brought 'down a peg or two' and judged harder.

The 2016 Dove Global Beauty and Confidence Report studied 10,500 women and showed that women's beauty confidence was on a steady decline regardless of age or geography.[38]

PAUSE FOR A MOMENT AND REFLECT
How did you perceive the Beauty Load for those
deemed the 'beautiful ones'?

The Beauty Load has evolved to be felt by all of us as an internal struggle of not-enough-ness. What does this internal struggle look like? That's exactly what we'll explore in Part II.

Part II

What is the Beauty Load doing to us?

THE BURDEN OF IT

'There are no photos of me. I don't let anyone take any because I don't want to be seen like this.'

'I never put my hand up to speak in meetings as I don't want everyone to look at me and see how horrible I look.'

'I never let anyone, not even my husband, see me naked. The lights are off and I am under the covers before my clothes come off.'

The above are all comments from women in my network.

Do you have obsessive thoughts, rituals or rules for your beauty? Constant thoughts and noise in your head about the way you look? Yes? You are not going crazy. Well, you might be, but at least you are not alone! This way of thinking is hard to avoid in this fast-paced world that favours head over heart. And then add to that the Beauty Load! It kind of makes us all a bit cray-cray.

Women (and men) across the Western world are unwittingly playing into the pressures of the Beauty Load in the millions by feeling negative and critical of themselves and the way they look.

The following chapters explore some of the more internal negative side effects that the Load is having on us.

Firstly, we will explore the consequences of the Beauty Load on us personally.

Secondly, we will explore the consequences of the Beauty Load on our intimate relationships.

All of it starts in our heads, so let's go there first.

FROM MY NETWORK

What conditions and experiences make you feel less beautiful?

- 'When my husband doesn't tell me I'm beautiful.'
- 'Hanging out with beautiful young people.'
- 'Seeing the creases and wrinkles everywhere and realising this is just going to get worse.'
- 'When I am unhappy.'
- 'Being around young females in thong bikinis or that have no body fat makes me feel less beautiful.'
- 'When I spend too much time looking through social media at made-up girls with so much work done it's unfair to everyone else.'
- 'Trying on bikinis.'
- 'Civilisation.'
- 'Being on the beach.'
- 'Looking at myself in the mirror.'
- 'Clothing that doesn't fit, not being able to create an outfit that looks good, bad hair days, definitely bathing suits (ugh!).'

Chapter 9

The protective parts of us

What do you need to do to feel confident enough to wear a bikini at the beach or pool?

- Lose a few kilos?
- Shave your legs?
- Wax your bikini line?
- Do a hundred sit-ups a day for the week prior?
- Buy a new bikini (plus beach dress, sunglasses and hat)?
- Put on some fake tan?
- Or just get the latest muu-muu-style coverall so that not a millimetre of your skin is showing?

You might worry about how your body will look to your friends, or whoever you are going to the beach with, but that is often not where it ends. If it stopped with how you looked in front of the people you know, you would probably feel far less anxious and skip off to the beach alone on the regular. But you may also worry—and this sounds kind of crazy when you say it out loud—about all the other people at the beach who will see you and what they will think of you and the way you look.

These are not people that you care about. You will never meet them again, nor do they have any influence over your life.

But you worry what they are thinking as you walk down to the water's edge without your towel or other coverings. You want to be seen as beautiful by them or next to them. This pressure seems even more intense if they are looking the way you wish you looked.

I know it's not just me who feels this judgement from strangers. One of my friends avoided going to the beach from the age of nine years old until she was in her twenties. Another friend got an excuse note for every swim class at high school, and it wasn't because she didn't like swimming. Women say no to activities that are otherwise joyous, such as swimming at the beach, so as not to be seen.

PAUSE FOR A MOMENT AND REFLECT
How do you feel at the beach?
What activities do you opt out of in order for
your body not to be seen?

Statistics show that body image issues in adolescent girls are holding them back from seemingly unrelated activities, such as putting their hand up in class, going on school camp or playing sport—all because they worry that they do not look good enough.[39] And it's not for a fashion show or the school formal, it is something much more important: it is to have an opinion and take up space in class. Research shows that seven out of ten girls with low body esteem will not stick to their decisions or be assertive in their opinions. Eeek!

Just like my friends not partaking at the beach or the pool, women do this too and not just in swimmers. We say no to standing up, showing up, speaking up, fun things, satisfying things and things that connect us to who we really are.

Here's my interpretation of what's happening. We get so used to worrying about how other people view us that we start to see ourselves and our body through other people's eyes. It is as though we have disassociated from the internal experience of living in our body and we are outside of our bodies looking back at ourselves through the critical, judging eyes of some pieced-together authority figure (part mum, part teacher, part cool/mean girl) to find our faults.

We are looking at ourselves at the beach in the bikini as though we are being seen by our worst critic, noticing all the bad bits and being all judgey. No wonder we feel uncomfortable.

Seeing ourselves from the outside like this brings us under the influence of our protective parts, sometimes known as the inner critic or the ego. As mentioned in Chapter 5, these protective parts have an important job to do, and that is to keep us safe. In our modern world, safe no longer means 'able to run away from the predator' as it did for our ancestors, but it still means belonging, which is wired into our brains in the same way it was for those savanna-dwelling ancestors of ours.

THE PRIMAL NEED TO BELONG

The wiring in our brains has not changed much since prehistory, despite the massive changes in our way of life. It is still so important for us to fit in and belong to our family, in our community and with a life partner.

Belonging as a primal need is a psychological lever that has broad consequences.[40] Our interests, motivation levels, general health and happiness are all inextricably linked to the extent to which we feel we belong to a broader community. Even a single instance of exclusion has the power to lower our IQ, undermine our wellbeing and impede our capacity for self-control. This explains, to some degree, the heightened reactions and sense of doom and panic that our nervous system plummets into when there is the merest whiff of rejection. It could mean isolation and therefore, for the wiring in our brains, danger.

As women, we receive daily messages that looking good is important. Magazine headings do their best to encourage us towards external perfection. 'Get the bikini body!' they cry. 'Clear skin in three days!' they promise, egging us on to not be satisfied until we look that way.

I'LL BE HAPPY WHEN …

Have you ever said the words, 'I'll be happy when …'? Maybe it's when 'I lose another three kilos' or 'get lash extensions' or 'get rid of this blemish'. This language is a sign that we believe our happiness is out there waiting for the ducks to get lined up in a row all perfectly. It is the promise of happiness through getting our surface selves sorted.

PAUSE FOR A MOMENT AND REFLECT
How do you finish the sentence,
'I'll be happy when …'?

Do you feel happy when you get the result you were chasing? Or do the goal posts keep moving?

This is us looking at our bodies through those external eyes again. The critical external-authority-figure view of ourselves gets us stuck under the influence of our protective parts. And this, make no mistake about it, is not generally a kind or reasonable influence. The protective parts of you don't care about how you feel—that is not in their job description. Their only job is to keep you safe. Safe from shame, rejection, embarrassment and failure, and they will go to any lengths, any nasty thought, any crippling self-belief to save you from this perceived danger.

If we are (in our minds) looking at ourselves through the eyes of some abstract, judgemental external authority, we are putting ourselves at the mercy of a mean voice. This voice has an influence that over time spirals us into shame and disgust. It takes us out from being inside ourselves, here, present with our inner experience. It takes us away from being in our bodies and experiencing life, which, importantly, means we are not able to enjoy life fully.

WE DO NEED TO BE SAFE

We need to belong, but we are all out of whack. Don't you think? The Beauty Load encourages us to look at the surface and feel judged based on looks regardless of whether the people that matter to us are actually judging us or not. Our protective parts encourage us to focus on fitting in. The problem is not that we have these vigilant protective parts, but that we are way out of balance. To find balance, we need to nourish and energise our inner world and find our Self. We need to remind ourselves that we are safe. We need to feel and experience the world inside, in our hearts, and come back into our bodies, our senses and the present.

Even as I write this, I place my hand on my heart. Being centred here means to come home to our body, our Self. The more we activate our internal Selves, the more we find the confidence we have been seeking. The more we can partake in activities, go to the beach, stick to our decisions and share our ideas.

To sum up, seeking our happiness in our external looks puts us at the mercy of the critical voice of our protective parts, and this is not working for us at all. It is not only a mean influence, but generally has us disconnected from the present, our bodies and our true Selves.

PAUSE FOR A MOMENT AND REFLECT
What happens when you take a deep breath
and focus on how it feels to be you,
rather than how you look?

Chapter 10

We feel a shame shitstorm

One day after school when I was about fifteen, I was sitting at the bus stop waiting to go home, watching the private school boys file off the bus past me. I was at the peak of my awkward adolescent phase. To add to my flat chest, I had braces, pimples, a bad haircut, and constantly flushed cheeks. I didn't feel attractive and it was obviously tangible because the boys noticed and responded in kind. On this particular day, as they filed past me, they hit me with a shame grenade.

One of them looked straight at me, with his gaggle of disciples hanging on his every move, and said quite simply 'Eww, yuck!' The disciples giggled in agreement as they walked away, probably never thinking of this moment again. For me, however, it wasn't so easy to forget.

I wanted to be swallowed up by the ground beneath me and disappear. In that moment and in many moments that followed, I felt utter humiliation and shame about how I looked.

One thing the Beauty Load makes us feel, more than anything else, is shame.

Shame leaves us with an intense feeling of wanting to hide—which ironically, as Brené Brown describes in her book *The Gifts of Imperfection*, only makes it worse.

Brown explains that shame exists in secrecy. It thrives on being hidden and buried, where it grows and 'metastasises'.

'Shame cannot survive being spoken,' Brown says. 'It cannot tolerate having words wrapped around it. What it craves is secrecy, silence, and judgement. If you stay quiet, you stay in a lot of self-judgement.' It hates it when we share it or tell its story; she says, 'it can't survive being shared.'

The more our shame is hidden and locked away, the more it intensifies and thrives (and gets us stuck in our ruminating negative heads).

When it comes to the Beauty Load, hiding our shame often looks like hiding our bodies. There are so many ways to hide. Some of us hide our size under layers of clothes, our skin under make-up, our stature with high heels, our teeth by keeping our mouth closed. For me, as I mentioned earlier, it was hiding behind my push-up bras. I hid by numbing my senses with alcohol, by drawing attention to my legs and away from my chest, by projecting my discomfort onto others, by running away from intimate moments—tactics that we'll explore in later chapters.

PAUSE FOR A MOMENT AND REFLECT

What part of you does shame make you want to hide?
How do you hide yourself or your body?

Dr Mario Martinez, in his book *The MindBody Code: How to change the beliefs that limit your health, longevity, and success,* talks about shame being cultural. He says that shame is the force that keeps us toeing the cultural line. Its aim is to improve us, change us, and trim off the less desirable bits so that we do fit in. We know the rules because the culture raised us, teaching us its shame language from a young age.

The culture dictates many aspects of our life by imposing its beliefs on us—the guidelines for when to couple up and have children, how menopause will go, when middle age is, how long we will live and much more. If you are still, for example, 'on the shelf' five years after the culture tells you to be married, you will feel the hot burn of shame.

Yet, culture is diverse with different culture 'shame pressures' among families, regions and peoples. In the case of the Beauty Load, despite there being different rules from place to place, it is felt widely across the globe.

If you step out of line within your culture, you could be punished with shame, which has serious implications not just on your social standing but also on your wellbeing. Shame gives us that telltale desire of wanting to shrink or disappear in a puff of smoke, as I did at the bus stop that afternoon.

Shame felt due to the Beauty Load is hard to avoid. We are asked to toe the beauty line in so many ways.

FORMS OF BEAUTY LOAD SHAMING

There are many different ways we can feel shame about our body and looks. You may have felt one or many of the following.

1. Family beauty shame

You know if you are not fitting the family beauty expectations. If you put on a few extra kilos, you might be teased; if you wear a skirt that is too revealing, you get the 'eye roll'; and if you don't scrub up well enough for a family gathering, you will be verbally slapped down.

Shame is a tool that is used in families, whether consciously or not, to keep its members in line. As parents, it helps to be conscious of any shaming we direct towards our kids. Seemingly small comments like 'Are you sure you should be eating that?' are sometimes all that it takes. These comments often come from our own fear of our beloved family members putting on weight or looking *less than ideal* to the world; we are worried about the consequences they may have to face. Yet, in shaming them, we are saying 'You are only okay if …'—words that have the power to create lifelong body image stories for our loved ones.

2. Generational beauty shame

What was your mother's relationship like with her body? What about your grandmother's? (You may need to look at your male lineage too).

Was she free and happy in her beauty? Was she confident in her body? Did she enjoy the pleasure it brought her?

Or was she constantly critical, always on diets, and needing to change, prune or fix her natural state of being?

What comments did you receive from well-meaning family members about your body growing up?

PAUSE FOR A MOMENT AND REFLECT
What body shame did you inherit from your
mother (or other family)?
How has this inheritance affected you?

3. Religious beauty shame

Whether you are a follower of a religious tradition or not, you probably feel its influence when it comes to beauty. Across the board, most religions around the world have a narrative that tells us that women must be pure, chaste, pious and even saintly. This is where beauty and sex weave together to become one shame influence. Dressing up, looking alluring and bringing out your most attractive assets are far removed from the purity of the nun's habit. The more pious and 'good' you are perceived by your religion, the less you focus on your looks and your attractive appeal.

This may have helped women avoid the Beauty Load to some degree if they were willing to toe the purity line, but for those who didn't, there was shame.

Historically (and still to this day), the church, the mosque and the temple did not want women to look so available as to tempt its male congregation, as this would have had social impacts on its constituents—impacts ranging from distraction to lineage and ownership tussles. After thousands of years of influence over their populations, our culture is thick and heavy with the remnants of this shame, whether we adhere to a religion or not.

4. General public beauty shame

You will know this kind of general, public humiliation if you have ever stepped out into the world without adhering to the cultural standards.

General public shaming can come in response to:
- our shape
- our race
- our age
- our grooming—body hair, odour, etc.
- our presentation choices and identity—do we look slutty, scruffy or dangerous?
- our wealth—can we afford these beauty rituals or those nice clothes?

- our ability—are we disabled or scarred?
- our sexuality or gender

5. Fat shame

A client of mine reports that when she was slim, she was shocked at how differently she was treated to when she was bigger. As a slim woman, she noticed that people were kind, welcoming and friendly, whereas as a bigger woman, she feels invisible or looked down upon.

Cultural attitudes about bigger bodies have been shaped by the images we see online, but also by government ad campaigns and medical advice. In the 1990s in Australia, there was a 'war on obesity' campaign telling us to stop eating sugar, get fit and stop being a drain on our families and the medical institutions.

Studies have shown that obese people on average receive at least one negative interaction every day. Every day! The general attitudes towards bigger-bodied people are: *You are lazy, You eat too much* and *You don't look after yourself* ... in essence that it is their fault and they should do something about it.[41]

6. Racial shaming

Australia can be a whitist, racist place despite the fact that we are a diverse, multicultural nation, with nearly thirty per cent of us born overseas, and despite the fact that white settlement is only fairly recent in the history of this land and its people.[42]

A 2019 study found that forty per cent of Australian school kids from non-anglo or European backgrounds experience racial discrimination from their peers.[43] Discrimination ranging from being called names to being subjected to violence (and this is school kids!).

7. Media beauty shame

The ads, in showing us the generic, collated, photoshopped, improved versions of women, shame us. They show us the before and after pics of a weight loss program, or a hairy 'embarrassing' leg followed by a smooth, slender, beautiful version. Suddenly, our 'before shot' bodies or our bodies that are of different colour, race, ability or size and not even represented, feel shameful. This message might not affect us so much if we were only exposed to it occasionally, but with estimates being that we are exposed to over four thousand ads a day, the idea that our body is in some way shameful becomes less like something we can consciously ignore and more like something that is so familiar it becomes fact.

8. Woman-to-woman beauty shame

Women can be our own harshest critics. We make comments to each other such as, 'I really like that TV presenter but what the hell is she thinking with that jacket?' With our catchphrase often reduced to a simple 'What was she thinking?' we can cut a woman down in a single comment about her bad hair, weight gain, fashion faux pas or unfortunate facelift. Have you noticed that we are much harsher on other women than we are on men? We expect the beauty standard to be upheld by women and we are ready to hurtle a shame grenade at them if they stuff up.

Woman to woman, shame can be harshest when we get together with our friends. Not that we would ever purposely want to make our friends feel bad, but because in complaining and lamenting about our own perceived flaws, we can cause a comparison shame attack for our friend.

Have you ever had a friend:

- who was slimmer than you complain about her weight gain?
- who had fewer blemishes than you lament her one pimple?
- who had bigger breasts than you wallow about her small bust? (Okay, that was my own personal example there!)

When this happens you think sometimes out loud, but often in your head, *So if that little thing makes you that upset, you really must think that I am unacceptable.* Prior to this, you may have felt okay about yourself, but now you are second-guessing yourself and your acceptability.

Woman-to-woman shaming is a kind of grandiosity. Relationship expert Terry Real explains that while shame is what happens when contempt is turned inwards on ourselves, grandiosity is when that contempt is turned outwards towards others. While shame makes us feel unworthy and 'one down', grandiosity gives us reprieve, putting us momentarily 'one up' so that we feel entitled and superior. All the shame of comparisons, the media and the beauty ideals have us feeling so shit that we look for relief with the grandiose tall-poppy syndrome, racism, fatism, or woman-to-woman shaming, making us feel superior and less unworthy for a moment.

To recover from both shame and grandiosity, Real says we need to be eye-to-eye with our fellow humans: not above, not below. We need to be okay with being messy, imperfect, 'warts and all' humans with a bunch of other messy warts-and-all humans.[44]

Do you notice the grandiose woman-shaming
moments in yourself?
Have you ever felt shamed by other women
in relation to beauty?
How does it feel when others make themselves
superior to you?

9. Self beauty shame

We are harder on ourselves than we are on anyone else, don't you think? Our protective parts think that the self-criticism is helping us, motivating us to do the work of beauty so that we fit in, but overall it just makes us feel shit about ourselves. Self-shame steals our joy. It is contempt turned inwards, making us feel sick.

Let's take our relationship with food as just a small example of how we shame ourselves. Do you casually feel able to relish the pleasure of eating delicious food like cheese, ice cream or chocolate fudge brownies? I'm guessing, perhaps, you don't. Instead, you likely hear the harsh jibes of your inner critic, shaming you for going to the fridge, shaming you for being hungry, shaming you for wanting what you 'shouldn't want' because it is going to 'make you fat'. *Fat!*—which has become one of the most shameful labels of all, where the cultural narrative in our heads starts instantly deeming ourselves unworthy of feeling beautiful or even of being included. When this shaming comes from within yourself, it can feel like evidence that you are the problem rather than the toxic culture that cultivated this in you.

10. Tall-poppy beauty shame

When I was growing up, saying that you thought you were beautiful or pretty was a sure-fire way to get harshly torn down and told that you were, as we say here in Australia, 'up yourself'. These days I applaud my fellow women who claim their beauty, but this might still be very uncomfortable. We have been culturally programmed to play it 'safe' and instead of noticing and enjoying our beauty and all that we love about ourselves, we highlight our so-called 'faults'. This has become so ingrained in us that we start to truly believe the shame story, and often feel much more comfortable giving our 'problem areas' the limelight than claiming our beauty amongst others.

I do see this changing for the gen Zs. Selfie culture and social media has shifted things. Bachelorette and TV host Abbie Chatfield posts selfies of herself in a skimpy dress with the caption 'hot'. The younger generation are owning it and changing the rules.

11. Shame for caring about the Beauty Load

Here's the irony. We feel shame about the way we look but we also feel shame for feeling the Beauty Load itself. Taking time to get ready to go out, spending too much money (and too much of our free time) on clothes and beauty, and wanting the good light or the right angle to take a photo (and then wanting a reshoot or deleting the photo altogether), feel slightly silly.

So even caring about how we look feels shameful. Lauren Shields in her book *The Beauty Suit* explains this: 'Vanity is unseemly because how one looks is supposed to be unimportant, and obsession with something so frivolous is worthy of ridicule.'[45] Yet we also receive the message—on loop—that there is nothing more important than looking good.

We would like to think that we are confident and stable enough within our own self-image not to care. We feel silly and adolescent, especially as fully grown adults, about the negative thoughts that run through our heads. We feel silly as we know that there are people struggling with the Load worse than us and because there are bigger problems in the world. Feeling silly about it doesn't make the problem go away. On the one hand, it just adds to the heavy Load we carry, keeping us stuck from really processing and dealing with it, and on the other it shows how difficult and contradictory our attempts to look good and fit in are.

PAUSE FOR A MOMENT AND REFLECT
What shame have you felt in relation
to the Beauty Load?

Shame works at informing you of a family or a society's ideals and expectations and keeping you in line with that. Shame works, albeit at a terrible cost to our self-esteem, at creating a feeling of unworthiness that marketers can use as a tool to make us spend money and buy stuff. Shame **does not work** when it comes to bringing out our best selves.[46] Shame does not motivate us. It makes us feel worse about ourselves. It holds us back from sharing our ideas, having a fun day at the beach or participating in life. It has us obsessively cover up our flaws or hide away from life and living, whilst reaching for comfort and feeling hopeless.

The body positivity movement is great. It tells us every human deserves to feel positive about their body no matter how well it fits the shape, size, colour or ability of the cultural ideal. But at times, the message can feel impossible. 'Love your body', it says. Loving your body in a culture that tells you to find it disgusting, and that safety is in conforming to the ideal, is not that easy. Not being able to love your body could in fact add to the shame; 'I can't even do that right,' we say to ourselves, taking it as further proof that we are beyond salvation.

Loving your body in this culture obsessed with looks is not easy.

Another movement has emerged, which may be an easier transition: body neutrality. This movement encourages us not to love our body but to *feel neutral about it*—neither negative nor positive—and not to think too much about it, basically just get on with our lives. Just get on with life … that sounds like what a lot of men do.

Let's think neutral to get out of shame.

Because shame sucks, and here is an even bigger problem. Not only does shame make us feel shit about ourselves, and make us want to change ourselves or hide away, but it also has us wanting to hide the very fact that we feel the Beauty Load.

When feeling the Beauty Load feels like shame, we hide this from each other. We do this because we start to believe that this constant stress, pressure and worry that we feel about our looks is personal. We think that feeling the Load is proof that we are flawed, that it is a result of our own particular body imperfections, which in turn makes us want to hide our experience of the Load even more. We don't want our friends and family to know that we are so 'flawed' that we feel the Beauty Load. Not sharing it makes it feel easier to cover up, but remember what Brené Brown says … it only metastasises it.

The truth about the Load is that it is not personal; it is not, in fact, about **our** looks. It is not about us!

The Beauty Load creates a shame grenade and its effects on us are toxic. We will talk more about how to escape that shame in Chapter 22.

Chapter 11

We don't feel good enough

When I was a young woman, the story of 'I am not attractive' was so deeply entrenched in my psyche that it became the filter through which I saw myself in the world.

I seemed to always find more reason to believe that my story was true. Even the slightest negative reaction would be notched up as evidence. If a man turned away from me, made a comment about my hair colour ('You know what they say about redheads?' No, I really don't), or just did not notice me at all, I saw it and added the experience to my list of evidence that I was not attractive. When I look at photos of my younger self now, it seems ridiculous. Now, I see a beautiful young woman in her physical prime and it feels like such a shame that I couldn't enjoy it.

But here is what I have realised; it is impossible to look at a woman and size up her beauty insecurity by her external appearance. This may seem contradictory to the preordained beauty checklist that I mentioned earlier in the book, but as we will discuss in this chapter, the Beauty Load is more complex than it seems and full of contradictions.

The Beauty Load is not so much about our body, but more about our beliefs. Beliefs that stem from our history and experiences: comments, exposure, traumatic events, responses, presumptions and rejections. All of which have the capacity to kick off our beauty insecurity.

I know a woman who struggles with the Beauty Load even more than most. Of course, looking at her, it seems incomprehensible, but that is the quirk of the Beauty Load. For this woman, it all started at a party one night when she was in her late teens. A boy who she had been flirting with, and who she knew fancied her, turned on her. Once he was with his peers and fuelled by alcohol, he started laughing about the impossibility of being with her, shaming her and setting off a belief in her that she was unattractive and laughable. This resulted in a spiral of insecurity in her mind that she is still struggling to shake now as an adult.

I call it the perfect storm of insecurity. A kind of explosion of beliefs and events that create the foundations of not feeling beautiful enough.

It happens when the following three factors combine:

1. We get the message that beauty is the key to belonging.

From the day we are born, little girls are clucked over and told they are pretty. We learn from the get-go that the way we look is a sure-fire way to get attention and gain approval. Our focus on looks becomes tied into being worthy and we become vigilant, looking out for this approval (or its opposite) everywhere.

2. We get the message that the ideal beauty is out of reach for us.

We see the visions of beauty, but we realise in the harsh light of day that we don't look like that, mainly because what we are seeing is airbrushed, photoshopped and often not humanly possible.

This was very much a message that I had as a youngster. I was teased at school, called 'freckle face' and 'ginger nut'. It did not fill me with a sense that I was pretty in any of the right ways.

3. An adolescent shitstorm of negative messaging.

We get hit in our vulnerable teenage years with society's expectations of how we need to measure up to be good enough, usually in the form of paranoia, coincidence and a barrage of Beauty Load messages. The teenage years are an important developmental stage. It is the stage where we expand our vistas, looking up and out from our family unit and beyond to find our identity in belonging with our peers. It is a stage where a lot of growth is happening in our brains, and more than ever we want to fit in.

For the woman mentioned earlier, the shitstorm was the event at the party where she was laughed at. For another, it was the shame of being bullied and told by the hot guy that he wouldn't have sex with her even if she 'paid him'. For some, it is taunts, rejection and put-downs from friends or parental figures. For me, the shitstorm (or one of them) was the comment by the boys filing past me off the bus.

The perfect storm of insecurity leaves us feeling broken, ugly, despondent and lost. In this environment, beliefs start to form about ourselves; that we are not enough, that we are ugly, unattractive, unlovable and very much in need of fixing. It is a ripe and fertile environment for insecurity.

PAUSE FOR A MOMENT AND REFLECT
Did you experience a perfect storm of insecurity?
What were the influential factors that created it for you?
What body image belief were you left with as a result?

The perfect storm caused us pain and insecurity. Insecurity makes us feel shit about ourselves but it is not trying to mess up our life, it is trying to keep us safe. Insecurity is another protective part. It is trying its hardest to save us from pain, trying to keep us 'safe' from being rejected, bullied and belittled and feeling unworthy. Let's take a moment to see what insecurity is doing.

INSECURITY'S AIM IS TO HELP US AVOID PAIN

Pain could come from having unmet expectations, so insecurity smashes our expectations down.

Pain could come from putting ourselves out there and being vulnerable, so insecurity tells us to stay small and try nothing.

Pain could come from thinking we are beautiful, only to be told by others that we are not and then be deemed arrogant or 'up yourself!' So, insecurity keeps our expectations in check to the point of negativity.

Pain could come from getting really, super keen on somebody and then losing them, so insecurity tells us to stay aloof (hello cool girl!) or solo.

PAUSE FOR A MOMENT AND REFLECT

How has insecurity tried to keep you safe?

Unfortunately, insecurity sometimes doesn't have the safety effect it is hoping to have. The irony is that in our attempts to stay safe, our insecurity has us act and behave in ways that are reactive and fearful and often seem overly sensitive or downright weird to others. Insecurity, if we let it become too powerful, brings us the very things that it was created to avoid: rejection and isolation. Dealing with our insecurity can be counterintuitive. When we tell it to bugger off and hate on it, it becomes more powerful, whereas insecurity softens when we offer it understanding and support.

We tend to navigate our insecurities by squaring the balance in our own way, whether that be telling ourselves that we don't 'give a shit' about how we look; giving up on trying to be 'beautiful'; opting out of getting involved in life; or directing our attention to sports, creativity or our careers to compensate.

The Beauty Load often has us wondering *Am I pretty enough?* and feeling insecure. It isn't that we are insecure people; feeling the Load and worrying about how we fit in is inevitable with the cultural messages that abound. Let's say that again: it is not that we are insecure; the culture creates the problem.

The culture is the problem, not you.

Our job, unless we can go live in a cave in a mountain to avoid the culture, is to transform the struggle into something that feels more balanced, manageable and healthy for us—which we will talk about more about in Part III.

Chapter 12

We become body dysmorphic

Have you noticed that the Beauty Load makes us harder on ourselves than we are on others? I have already posited that we are tougher on other women than we are on men, but in the judgement hierarchy, we save the highest rung for ourselves. What would be fine and inoffensive on others, can often feel shameful to us. The upwards comparison that the Beauty Load instils in us has us expecting to be the image of perfection, and anything 'beneath' that feels like an embarrassing failure. Sometimes, in the worst cases, this sense of failure can even become life-threatening.

A few years back, I had a client suffering from severe depression. When we peeled away the emotional layers, the roots of her depression led us back to a self-hatred fuelled, in large part, by her 'ugly' mouth. For this woman, the way she looked had become so despicable to her that her life did not seem worth living.

This is an extreme case, but our obsession with how we look is creating a tendency towards body dysmorphia among women. Body dysmorphia is the mental disorder in which people see their own body or parts of it as flawed and obsessively cover up the flaw with various behaviours.[47] The classic example of this is anorexia, sufferers of which see themselves as too big, even when they are skeletal and dying. I see degrees of body dysmorphia in my friends too, albeit not as serious as anorexia.

My friends seem beautiful to me. They each have a natural radiance, something undeniably and individually attractive. The Self that I love in them shines through their external appearance. However, I realise that for many of them, their beauty is not such an easy thing to accept.

My friend Andrea, for example, is beautiful. When I have told her she is beautiful in the past, she has said, 'I know I am not and that's okay. I have come to terms with it.'

For her, a lack of beauty has become a fact. It has been wired into her in this way since high school when she was hit by the adolescent shitstorm of negative messages. Back then, it was a time when she was slightly over her happy weight and didn't quite fit in; she was bullied by the mean girls and was made to feel ugly and repulsive. The result is her own version of body dysmorphia, a belief that she is bigger and less attractive than she really is. She is reminded of this when she goes shopping, often heading to the change room with clothes two sizes too big.

Another girlfriend Chris turns heads as you walk down the street with her. Yet she doesn't feel beautiful either. Chris is fixated on her belly. From my perspective, as a mother of two children with a stretched tummy, I asked her, a woman who has not had children, quite genuinely, 'What are you talking about? Your belly is so flat you could model a bikini on the front of a magazine!'

'It sticks out,' she argued.

I can't see it, but she can. She is stuck in an obsessive discomfort with her tummy to the point where she would rather not go to the beach for fear of it 'sticking out' in front of friends or strangers with 'better bodies' than hers.

And these two aren't isolated examples. It's the norm.

My friend Jess hates her nose.

Jenny, her hairy arms.
Sarah, her big feet.
Kara, her thin hair.
Ani, her 'chunky' thighs.
Mish, her small eyes.
Neo, her 'wonky' teeth.
Sal, her scar.
Petra, her size.
Sigh. How can my beautiful friends not feel beautiful?

PAUSE FOR A MOMENT AND REFLECT
What beauty struggles do you notice
your friends have?

The Beauty Load blinds us to our actual beauty and zooms our attention in on our supposed flaws. It makes me sad. Sad because I see how the Beauty Load weighs my friends down, holds them back and wastes their time and potential, making them worry about how they look, when how they look is fine. It is **totally** enough and does not need to be a problem.

From over here, through my eyes, the eyes of a friend who loves them, it seems ridiculous. The truth is that I do see the things that they are complaining about—the nose, the thighs, the teeth, the scars—but for me it is all part of who they are. It is not ugly. It is them. Part of the package that I see as whole and beautiful. I love that they are different to the generic picture of beauty. I don't want 'model' perfect friends; in fact, I would probably be less comfortable with them if they were, as I certainly am not model-perfect. I don't want them to be a clone; I love that they are different and diverse. It makes life interesting.

To be a good friend, you do not have to be beautiful or perfect. That is not what I look for in my friends. What I look for is a good vibe when I am with them.

In knowing that my friends can't see or enjoy their own beauty, I realise that I too possess the critical filter of the Beauty Load. I must also see myself more harshly than others do.

If everyone I know is saying that they are not enough, and it is clear to me that they are enough, then my own perceived faults must be just as inconsequential to those who love me. What does it matter that my breasts are flat? If it doesn't matter to those who love me, why should it matter at all? Who am I imagining that it matters to?

Let's take a moment to pause here and recognise that we are more than likely harsher on ourselves than anyone else. That through eyes other than our own harsh authoritarian-critical-mean-girl ones, we might actually be okay.

Imagine if we were talking to a friend. Would we talk to them the way our harsh inner critic talks to us? We wouldn't want our beloved friends to have to put up with that mean voice, would we? We would want them to see their beauty and let it be enough. We would want them to enjoy their bodies, not be weighed down by inner criticism.

If our friends shared the mean voice that was running through their head, we would want to interrupt it and stop that voice from doing any more damage. So, surely, we want the same for ourselves too.

What if we did the same for ourselves?

Imagine if we saw ourselves through the eyes of love, instead of the eyes of our harshest critic.

What if we had a boundary for ourselves that did not allow that authoritarian mean voice anymore. What if, when it came—which of course it is going to after all those years of automatic thinking and conditioning from the world around us—instead of letting the harshness run its course, we simply caught the voice mid-flow, mid-heartless, nasty spiel, and took a deep breath. We would let the voice know that we get it is trying to keep us safe and that we appreciate that. Instead of telling this voice we hate it and to go away, we offer it understanding and support. We ask it what support it would need so that it didn't feel scared and have to use that mean voice. Maybe it just needs reassurance.

Then—instead of seeing ourselves from the viewpoint of that mean voice, the external authority figure—we could imagine that we were looking at ourselves from the eyes of our heart. Looking at our body from love ... as a vessel for life, fun, sensuality, connection and adventures.

Let's try that now. Take a moment, take a deep breath, close your eyes and feel yourself looking at your whole body and whole being from your big, caring heart, as if your heart has eyes. It's not about what it sees so much as how it feels.

How does it feel for you? Stay there for a moment.

For a free guided meditation that takes you to a kinder, more loving heart eyed view of yourself, go to nicolemathieson.com/bookresources

Chapter 13

We focus on the negative

Recently I had a friend who kept commenting on how great my hair was. 'Really? I woke up with it like this!' was often my response, which, while true, no doubt just irritated her.

But hair, you see, is not really on my beauty radar. It is not something that I think too much about, because hair has never been an issue for me, whereas it was totally an issue for my friend. She was struggling with thin hair, which, much to her disappointment, had started falling out. So much so that she had taken to wearing a hairpiece.

When I had my hair shaved off (which I will tell you about in Chapter 18), I noticed that I felt less feminine and attractive. Obviously, my hair is important to how much I feel the Beauty Load, but when it is long and feminine, it does not attract my focus of attention. Mostly, I brush it in the morning, and it generally acts appropriately. But do I appreciate it? Not really.

PAUSE FOR A MOMENT AND REFLECT
How does your hair influence your sense of beauty?

HAS THE BEAUTY LOAD BLINDED ME TO WHAT MAKES ME FEEL GOOD?

As a relationship coach, I am often encouraging my clients to take up gratitude practices to help shift their focus off all that is irritating and frustrating them about their partners, and onto the good. It works wonders.

Our minds are naturally vigilant and negatively biased; hardwired this way to notice the problems as a strategy to keep us safe. Gratitude is the secret key that can make a change in attitude occur. Instead of our natural default of scanning the world for danger or problems, gratitude asks our brains to scan the world for goodness—thus, creating in us the opportunity to see the abundance, good fortune, beauty and support that surrounds us even amidst the other stuff.

Of course, this is relevant to our looks too.

WE ARE NEGATIVELY SKEWED

The things I had put on my 'lack' radar—my breast size, my freckly skin and my angular proportions—have been the focus of my attention. All the while I had not appreciated my effortless hair at all!

We all have parts of us that we don't like so much. Yet, the truth that we often forget about is that we also have other parts that we do like. All of us! In fact, very few of us have the complete package of 'supermodel tick-box perfection'. Sadly, for our Beauty Load-addled mind, we can't just pick and choose parts, cutting and pasting ourselves together like a photoshopped magazine cover page. We have to take the full package, the parts we love and the parts we don't, and do the best we can with it.

I remember hearing an interview with Elle Macpherson, my childhood beauty hero, years ago, in which someone asked her if she had any parts of her body that she didn't like.

'Of course, I do!' she replied.

'And what are they?' the interviewer pressed.

'Well, I am not telling you, as they will become a public focus. I am keeping them to myself.'

PAUSE FOR A MOMENT AND REFLECT
What are the parts of your body that you feel content with?
What are the parts that get your focus?

EVEN ELLE PERCEIVES HERSELF AS HAVING PROBLEM AREAS!

We all have those things about us that don't quite fit the culturally preordained beauty picture or our own high standards. But our negativity bias blinds us. We forget the parts that are fine. We plant two feet into the commitment of the critical voice that sees us as flawed, then we often go that step further and tell ourselves it makes us lacking and unworthy. When really, we have a mix. We have the lot. We are not just one thing but a beautiful, complex combination of all the things.

Chapter 14

We become depleted of money, time, energy and power

A Colombian friend once said to me, 'Show me an ugly woman and you are showing me a poor woman.' Initially, I felt shocked! Her frank suggestion that beauty can be bought had me reeling. She believed that beauty was something that you worked on and purchased.

For example:

- getting the hair styled, coloured, blow-dried, straightened, permed, etc.
- getting the eyebrows shaped
- getting lash extensions
- having hair lasered or waxed
- putting creams and ointments all over
- buying and then putting on make-up
- getting the skin tanned
- having the nails done; manicure, pedicure
- having a facial
- buying shoes, handbags and clothes
- and the list goes on …

My friend believed that if you did not have the signs of beauty, then you obviously did not have the money for it. This may be more noticeable in a country like Colombia, where the wealth gap is larger.

While it shocked me at first, the idea that beauty can be bought is not ridiculous at all. In fact, it is probably a more honest appraisal of where we are at—and not just in countries like Colombia, but in Australia too.

Think about what you would do if you had an important event to go to. You would quite possibly look in your wardrobe and on seeing nothing appropriate might, budget depending, go buy something. A new item or outfit could change the way you feel, your confidence being only one trip to the shops away. How you feel at an event or outing can all change with one new 'beauty saving' piece.

You can go from feeling very average to feeling full of confidence, like you belong, all with the simple exchange of money—which adds wealth and class to the beauty privilege intersections. What about the people who can't afford to dress up for the job interview?

Shopping is now the hobby of choice of millions of young women. Ask a group of teen girls in any Western country and most of them would put shopping up there as their favourite pastime.[48] With the global environmental crisis that we are facing and the fashion industry being the second largest global polluter after the oil industry, this is more than just a problem for our confidence.[49]

In my experience, the kneejerk response to the feeling that one is not beautiful is to go get something new. But I find that no matter how much I spend or how happy I am with my new purchases at the time, the confidence boost doesn't last long.

When I first get the confidence-saving item in my wardrobe, I get a buzz, and sling it on with glee. I go out wearing it with a spring in my step. But the next time I look in the wardrobe, the buzz has gone. There is no glee left, just a bunch of clothes that don't excite me and make me feel just as lacking as before. This is why the shopping sprees continue. The thrill is momentary. The search is endless; the fashion industry is always changing the goalposts so that I always feel like I need to catch up.

The Beauty Load is supporting an estimated $621 billion fashion industry, and this figure is only the womenswear sector of the fashion and textile industry.[50]

Beauty is an area in which our insecurities are turned into big bucks by the marketers. Shopping is not a hobby that holds its value. The value is lost pretty much immediately as fashions change and the buzz dies, and we are already looking to fill the hole and acquire that next piece and then the next and the next. It is classic ego-driven behaviour: the mind telling us a story that there is something missing, something not quite enough, something external that we can acquire to fill the hole and feel good about ourselves.

PAUSE FOR A MOMENT AND REFLECT
How often do you feel the pull to get something
new in your wardrobe?
How long does the new purchase make you feel good?
How much money are you spending on clothes? Money, let's
remember, that statistically speaking the men
(to a large degree) keep in their wallets.

BUT IT DOESN'T END THERE

How long does it take you to get ready to go out? How much *time* do you spend on your beauty? It is not just money that the

Beauty Load is stealing from us; it is also the minutes, hours and days, which really add up when you look back.

I have tried to avoid colouring my hair for many years; I simply couldn't afford it. More recently, I decided to go get some highlights in, a nice balayage of blonde to freshen me up. It took three hours! Three hours that I will never get back. Three hours that I was naively unprepared for and had me in a panic of school pick-up arrangements from the salon chair. It is a social norm for women to commit to this time (not to mention the expense) every six weeks or so. It is a choice, of course, but one that men do not have to make.

Time at the hairdresser, time shopping for an outfit, time doing make-up, time changing outfits a hundred times when you just can't find anything to wear ... if we added it all up, we might be shocked by how long we spend on our appearance. And lucky for us, somebody has done the sums. According to a 2014 study in the USA, over the course of twelve months women spend 355 hours on their hair and make-up alone. That's a full fourteen days per person per year on average.[51] A time loss that most men do not suffer; instead they can put this time towards other things such as career, leisure time and hanging out with family and friends.

Jia Tolentino, a feminist author, puts it like this: '[It's] as if some deep patriarchal logic has made it that women need to achieve ever-higher levels of beauty to make up for the fact that we are no longer economically and legally dependent on men.'[52] In other words, the freer we are in our society to be independent, the more the expectations of the Beauty Load keep us in chains.

More subtly than time and money, what effect does the Beauty Load have on our energy levels?

Ask any woman how she feels these days, and if she is being honest with you, she will tell you that she is exhausted. What with work, relationships, parenting, the mental and emotional loads we carry, and of course the Beauty Load, it feels like we are constantly switched on, worried and that there is just not enough time to relax and revive.

When our nervous systems are on constant alert, checking whether we are accepted and looking 'good enough', it has us in a perpetual state of hypervigilance, a state of being that activates our sympathetic nervous system and saps our energy. The insecure thoughts, the worry and the self-doubt come at the cost of our energy and thus our wellbeing.

If you think about it, when we are feeling sassy, confident and beautiful in our own skin, it's like we're tapping into a limitless source of energy and wellbeing. We vibe and we radiate. On the flipside, when we are worried and self-conscious, it is like we have a black hole sucking our energetic life force right out of us.

PAUSE FOR A MOMENT AND REFLECT
How is your energy these days?
Do you feel an undercurrent of stress
from the Beauty Load?

Stress around how we look is draining our energy.

Naomi Wolf reckons that this energetic depletion is a strategic construct of the patriarchy. She believes it is created out of political fear on the part of the male-dominated hierarchy of the threat of liberated, energised women.[53] The idea being that a depleted woman is more easily manipulated and distracted, and therefore less of a threat to the powers that be. I mean, what would the world be like with billions of liberated, energised women?

When you think about the Chinese foot-binding practices, it

is hard to deny the link between beauty and a power imbalance between men and women.[54] Foot binding first came about in the Tang Dynasty in the seventh century and remained until the twentieth century. It was the practice of girls having their feet wrapped to restrict growth, with the aim of making their feet as small as possible. Walking was difficult, so servants were needed to perform menial tasks and husbands were no doubt essential too for support. Tiny feet were seen as a sign of elegance, modesty, nobility and even eroticism. Was this to do with the fact that your woman can hardly walk, let alone run away if needed?

In Europe, women wore corsets—even when heavily pregnant—and could hardly breathe.

We might look at the women of history and feel sorry for them, with the extreme, uncomfortable and disempowering practices they needed to partake in to be considered attractive. But let's just take a moment and consider some of the things we do now. Are we so very different?

These days, women wear short, tight skirts that restrict our movement; long (often false) fingernails that restrict our dexterity, especially with computer keyboards (and phones); and if we really want to be sassy and sexy, we wear high heels, possibly stilettos (the higher, the sexier). These practices seen through the filter of the Beauty Load are desirable, but if we shifted our filter, would it be possible to see them as disempowering and submissive to our men? We can't run, be strong or really move at all; we need support, help, and faith in a big strong man to be okay.

It is all disempowering:

- the money we spend
- the time we take on all aspects of our beauty

- the restrictive adornments and fashions
- the pain that we withstand for fashion
- the personal energy depletion
- the endless loop of needing more
- the destruction of our main energy source, the planet

All of these practices make us more helpless and less capable. When we are distracted and weak like this, and our appearance is taking up so much of our focus and mental energy, we have a lot less to give and a lot less influence on the world around us. Whether it is cunning and strategic on behalf of the patriarchy or not, the Beauty Load is working to deplete us of our confidence, our resources and our energy that we could be using to play bigger in the world.

Chapter 15

We think we need fixing

More and more women are having cosmetic surgery to feel good about themselves.

As a woman who has struggled with a flat chest my whole adult life, I get it. I get that some women feel the need to get implants to feel confident in their bodies. I get that after feeling too small or flat, having a larger bust could change the way you feel about yourself. I get that for other women, it is a breast reduction, a nose job, liposuction, a tummy tuck, a facelift or botox.

I also get that it may not provide the transformation in self-worth that many of the recipients are seeking.

It is a tricky area. I am sure every single one of us has a view on cosmetic surgery and whether it is a good or a bad thing. Perhaps you have had some work done yourself or perhaps you know someone who has. Perhaps you have seen it transform a life in all the good ways, giving hope, confidence and courage; alternatively, like my friend's sister who had work done on the cheap in South East Asia, perhaps you have seen it create devastation. Obviously, cosmetic surgery has an important role for so many people after accidents, mastectomies, and other medical issues, but that's not what we're talking about here.

When I watched a documentary called *Under the Knife* by Louis Theroux, I was amazed when he spent time in LA, the plastic surgery mecca of the world, interviewing surgeons, patients and a woman with the job title of 'image consultant'. The image consultant was recommending that her patient transform herself through a series of surgical procedures, 'helping' the patient sculpt her body cosmetically to become more 'beautiful'. The patient didn't even know what she wanted to change but entrusted those decisions entirely to the consultant.

Pre-op, the client was taken to a Rodeo Drive boutique to try on clothes, where the consultant described how much better the clothes would look on her once her body was 'fixed'. The patient was excited about the surgery, saying, 'I want the surgery. These clothes, they're going to look perfect, like they're supposed to.'

One of the surgeons explained, 'In LA, women feel that nature got something wrong.' He goes on to say, 'I am just here to help women feel good about themselves.'

'Our bodies are wrong.'
'They need fixing!'
'There is a way that clothes are *supposed* to look.'

What the … ! I found this all highly disturbing.

The message that I received and was uncomfortable with was that, in order for us to 'feel good about ourselves'—i.e. sit in the right spot on the bell curve of perfection to fit into a world with (in my opinion) skewed vision—the answer was surgery. In other words, our bodies are wrong, and we need fixing.

Is it just me, or does this sound like brainwashing propaganda? The Beauty Load is leaving us unable to see ourselves or our bodies as enough. We are brainwashed by the hundreds and thousands of images we have seen. Brainwashed by our cultures' limited ideas of beauty, which are not even based on anything real. Brainwashed by the new 'normal' we see around us, which is not always real either. Brainwashed by the consultants and surgeons if we dare to let them get too close.

The cosmetic surgery industry is thriving; it was earning more than $27 billion by the end of 2016 and is growing rapidly.[55] And it seems that it is a self-perpetuating cycle, in that as more people play into the pursuit of perfection and get cosmetically altered, the less normal the rest of us feel and the more people feel the need to get surgically 'enhanced'. Kind of like how Mia Freedman thought there was something wrong with her eyelashes.

But then, if the surgery makes somebody feel happy and confident about themselves, isn't it a good thing? Sure.

The problem is not the women (and men) who opt for surgery to make themselves feel better, but the Beauty Load making us feel like there is something wrong with our bodies and that we need fixing.

PAUSE FOR A MOMENT AND REFLECT
Have you felt the urge or taken the plunge to have
surgery or cosmetic changes made to your body?
If so, what was it that made you want
to make the changes?

Perhaps it is back to the idea of trying to fit into the bell curve of normal, but not the broad middle part, instead the upper 'perfect' end of it. It is also back to the idea of feeling judged by an external authority figure and letting them decide what is right or wrong.

But here's the thing: we don't need anybody to tell us that we are okay. We don't need anyone or anything to validate the way we look. Not the nod of approval from an authority figure, parent, teacher or image consultant; not a man's attention; not a cool girl's embrace; not a version of our beauty being replicated to sell beauty and sex, therefore deeming us acceptable or in some way valuable.

In this culture, we have been encouraged all our lives to seek validation from an external source of authority. We check, *Am I right? Am I doing this right? Or am I wrong?* And it might be the case that there is a right and a wrong for certain things like science, mathematics and religion. In places where there are rules, like being a good Christian or following the laws of physics, it is exact: a matter of yes and no. But that is not the case when it comes to being you. You are the only one who can stand in your experience and say, 'This is right for me.'

Nobody else can validate your beauty. If you continue to need others' approval, you will continue to seek others' validation and acceptance until the day you die. You will continue to be stuck in your head, feel insecure and need to 'fix' things on the surface.

PAUSE FOR A MOMENT AND REFLECT
Do you feel like you need others' validation to
feel good enough?
If so, who do you tend to need the validation from?

The problem with fixing ourselves is that it often doesn't work. The self-worth and confidence issues that you are trying to fix or get away from don't disappear when you dabble on the surface. Instead, they morph and move, finding a whole new problematic focal point. If you find yourself wanting surgery, or you've had it and you still feel the same self-doubt, then it might help to do the deeper work too, and we will talk more about what that work might look like in Part III.

One of my role models, Turia Pitt, is an athlete who was in a terrible accident while running an ultramarathon in the Australian outback that left her with burns to over sixty-five per cent of her body. Turia is now a motivational speaker and author with a real knack for and a whole lot of experience in finding the right mindset. I stumbled upon her advice to others with facial disfigurations. It went something like this: if you are not worried about it, the person you are speaking to won't be worried about it either.

How others respond to you starts with your attitude, not the other way around. For now, until such a time that society shifts and we manage to diminish the Beauty Load and render it irrelevant, this is where it all starts. Living with grace and personal power around the way we feel about how we look. In other words, owning it.

THE BEAUTY LOAD AND INTIMACY

The following few chapters are an exploration of the effects of the Beauty Load on our intimate relationships and sex lives.

The Beauty Load can tell us that we are not good enough and mess with our heads, as we have explored in the past few chapters. This can have negative implications on our relationships.

We all want to feel safe and connected in our intimate relationships, yet when we are feeling unworthy, lacking or like we need fixing, it can set up belief systems that have us reacting and behaving in ways that interrupt our close connections. It can, for instance, have us run away from intimacy to avoid rejection; something that I have done all too often in my life, as you will see in the next few chapters.

Chapter 16

Dating and the Load

Dating is one of those times in our lives when the inner critic and the Beauty Load tend to combine to create a mega load.

Modern dating means sitting on your phone, swiping left or right after seeing the merest glance of an image on your screen. You are judging someone on their looks and presentation to either entice you to find out more or move on. A lot of pressure is put on the way those photos make the person look. As you make these superficial judgement calls, you know that other people are making the exact same judgement calls on you! You are being compared and rated on how you look and measuring your success by the amount of 'matches' you achieve (i.e. people who find you attractive who you have already liked). I can only imagine that this has you feeling either validated or rejected, depending on your results.

My dating life finished in 1996, well before online dating was a thing, so I called on my friends, my networks and my clients to fill me in on what it is like.

The consensus is that the pressure is on you having 'beautiful' photos. The quandary thus becomes: Do you use Photoshop and filters to make these photos the most 'stunning' version of you you can be, or do you trust the way you look naturally? Do you have your hair and make-up done? What happens when you meet in person? Do you even look like the image that you presented online?

A friend reported feeling pressure to 'measure up' to her photos when she eventually did get to the date.

Online dating focusses heavily on appearance. You don't read the bio first and then see the photo; it is image first every time. If you feel insecure about the way you look, it can be intimidating to say the least.

How do we cope with this much pressure on our looks? While the dating game may have changed, the way we respond to the intense pressure has not.

The Beauty Load can make us uncomfortable as we step into making ourselves available to date, and these are three of the tactics that we tend to use to cope that are not that healthy: Distraction, running away, and compensating.

DISTRACTION

For me, when I was single, I wanted desperately to find love, yet I found myself fully committed to believing my inner mean voice that said *Nobody will find you attractive.* The mega inner critic plus Beauty Load was all too much. I needed help getting beyond the sense of not being enough.

One way I found 'help' was to distract myself from my beauty insecurities was to get drunk. Getting drunk offered me freedom, permission and a brief reprise from my sense of lack. After a few drinks, I could let go of my perceived imperfections and my fear of inferiority, and maybe even feel attractive for a brief time. It felt exhilarating.

Thanks to alcohol, I was able to feel momentarily attractive. NB: Alcohol created many other problems for me over the years, so I am in no way glorifying its use.

Is it any wonder that so many dates take place within the

context of alcohol? For me, however, without a solid base of self-worth or my sober best judgement, alcohol had me attract the kinds of guys who didn't stay or tended to treat me poorly.

Many of us distract ourselves from our insecurities by numbing them out. We use an array of vices: booze, drugs, busyness, and increasingly, screens and devices. In doing so, we have become less able to be present with our own experience. If we have a minute spare, we don't tend to tune in to our inner voice that might help us pick up on cues such as red flags, or the feelings of discomfort that are inside. 'That voice doesn't make me feel good,' we reason. Instead, we distract from the discomfort by making it 'feel better'.

Distracting ourselves from being with our discomfort feels easier in the short term, but does not work for us long term, as we will discuss in Chapter 22.

PAUSE FOR A MOMENT AND REFLECT

What type of distractions have you used to overcome your insecurities when dating?

RUNNING AWAY

One of my clients reported that she just can't even imagine dating due to a scar on her face from surgery. Others have shared that they are tempted to give up on finding love entirely. Dating experiences leave them feeling anxious and hopeless, not because of the company, but because of the negative talk going on in their heads due in large part to the way they perceive they look. My clients are left wondering, *Why even bother? Nobody is going to find me attractive and the whole process is too hard and humiliating anyway.*

Running away is another tactic we use to escape the discomfort. Sometimes we run away or avoid intimacy entirely not just to escape ourselves and our pesky insecure thoughts, but to escape the terrifying consequences of getting close to someone. It doesn't stop at swiping, hooking up or dating because ... *what if I get close and then they realise that I am not enough?*

My dating informants report that it is quite common to get ghosted. They find a match online, they chat and get to know the potential suitor, then when things are heading towards actually meeting the person, the suitor disappears in a puff of smoke, leaving a trail of disappointment and confusion. The discarded party wonders what they had done wrong to create such a disappearance, and thanks to the Beauty Load, they tend to feel that they must just be not quite attractive enough. My guess is that it is nothing to do with the qualities or behaviour of you, the unmet date, but more a sign of terror for the ghoster. *Chatting—fine, but showing up? Eek! That could lead to rejection,* they might think to themselves (possibly subconsciously).

When I was young, and convinced I was lacking in the beauty stakes, I kind of did this ghosting thing too in my own way. One time I lined up a date, went over to his place feeling really keen, but terrified, and instead of leaning into the terror, I had an urge to escape rather than hang out for his proposed 'video watching with wine and snacks', which sounds so lovely! I opted to insist on driving his flatmate to the train station, leaving him standing at his front door wondering what the hell was going on. I never returned! I really liked him though, so go figure.

The running away tactic makes us seem allergic to pursuing our potential with anyone, even if we actually want it. The distance that running provides keeps us in our comfort zone, even though running away from the connection that our heart truly desires is not really comfortable at all. Running away is what happens when our fear wins over love. It is our protective parts again, convincing us that we are not enough, so that we don't do the dangerous thing of putting ourselves in the way of (eek!) rejection.

COMPENSATION

We compensate by trying to make ourselves 'better' than what we are, based on the idea that in our natural state we are not enough. The compensating could be purely concentrated on our appearance: spending hours getting ready; spending money on our hair, outfit or make-up; covering up; extending and pruning in order to be enough.

But we often compensate in other ways.

Before I met my husband, I was a tragic people pleaser. I would compensate for my lack of self-worth and the thought that I wasn't attractive by giving my love interests everything. I would become whoever I thought they wanted me to be. I would dismiss all of their red flags and I would put up with poor behaviour. This tactic never went well, and the 'relationship' would generally end in a flurry, with me in tears.

Statistics show that women with low self-esteem are more likely to stay in abusive relationships, which is beyond merely upsetting, not to mention dangerous.[56] The experience of abuse further degrades a person's low sense of self-worth, which can have the effect of entrenching them in the cycle of abuse and lack of trust in themselves that they are worthy of anything else or anything better. It can make it really hard to find the confidence or impetus to get out.

Any insecurity creates an opening for healthy relationships to be jeopardised. A lack of sharing, a false sharing, a compensation—these are all cracks for a lack of boundaries (on our part) and abuse (on theirs) to creep in.

There are always those parts of ourselves that we feel shame about. We might convince ourselves that this makes us the 'booby prize' and feel lucky that someone (anyone!) finds us attractive. In this state, we are on the back foot, not in a place of power, nor willing to share our true selves, our needs and our boundaries for risk of losing the connection. It is a vulnerable place to be.

The truth is that we all deeply desire to love and be loved. Our tactics, however, sometimes fly in the face of moving towards love.

My own focus on looks and the exterior parts of my body when I was dating made me wonder, was I actually seeking love? Why did I keep making choices from the disguise of oblivion? Why did I keep running away? And why did I feel I had to bend over backwards to make anyone hang around? I was left feeling worse about myself than ever.

In the realm of dating, we have to ask the question: Why do our looks matter so much? The partner we are seeking is not just a trophy husband/wife. We are not wanting to be someone's partner just because we are pretty enough to make their ego feel good. There are so many other important qualities to consider when we are deciding on a mate. If all those other qualities and values matter for us in a potential partner, then they must also matter for our potential partner when considering us.

The vision that I had of love was not purely superficial, so why was I imagining that my looks were all that my partner could see in me? In truth, I did not want a trophy man, nor did I want to be a trophy woman. I was really interested in what was beneath the surface. But it seems that I had become so focussed on how I may be judged on a surface level that I was only seeing others through the same narrow lens. A lens, that in truth, I despised.

Our protective parts want to keep us safe. Putting our hearts on the line, with the potential for rejection, seems too risky for some of our vigilant protectors. They hold us in the safety and comfort of the familiar but critical voice, holding us back, sabotaging our chances and keeping us out of love.

My protective parts can try to hold me out of love even now. If I let these parts have their way, they still don't want me to expose my flaws, or my most natural, vulnerable self. If we let our protective parts rule us, they will keep us in only the shallow waters of love and intimacy. Or worse, they will keep us out of the water entirely.

Once we are in a relationship, our protective parts do not disappear. In the next chapter, I will share with you how I projected my fear onto my husband in the form of anger.

Chapter 17

We project it onto our partners

The Beauty Load doesn't vanish once we find ourselves in a relationship.

In my marriage, depending on how I was feeling about myself, it seemed easy for the question of beauty to loom and dominate.

If my husband and I were having any kind of issue, in my mind as a kind of reflex, looks would become the *one major factor* that kept him with me: my attraction magnet. If I was not beautiful, my logic assumed, then the relationship would fall apart. I knew deep down that this was not true when I had an honest, soulful look at it, but the idea would pop into my psyche in moments of weakness and felt like the default setting for my deep-seated fears.

In these moments, it never occurred to me that my intelligence, kindness, personality, creativity, spirit or any other attribute was what attracted him to me. It was *always* my beauty.

The problem was that if I was not feeling attractive, I would start to mistrust 'us'. The more insecure I became, the more defensive and distrusting I would get with him, sometimes to the point of blame and anger. I would act out my fear with protest behaviour, pushing and testing to see if I could force a loving response from him. This (*newsflash!*) very rarely gave me the response I wanted.

One time when we were newlyweds, a couple of his friends from back home had come to Sydney for a visit. They were friends from back when he was going out with an ex-girlfriend, who he was with for years, an ex-girlfriend who I knew was pretty and had a great figure.

A gang of us went out for dinner together. It was fun hanging out and reliving old times over a few drinks. Then, at some point during the night, someone made a joking comment about his ex. It was something like, 'You could still be with her.' A joke, said in fun, perhaps even with a tone of sarcasm due to their obvious lack of compatibility, but I felt it like a blow to the heart.

In my head, there were stories running about all his friends not thinking I was as good as her. In my version of events, on the night, my husband had not come to my rescue like a good husband (read: knight in shining armour) should. In my version of things, what he should have said was, 'Nicole is such a better fit for me,' or something equally comforting.

From the moment that comment was made, the night was over for me. I retracted into my shell, fuming, and hardly spoke another word. When my husband and I were finally alone together at home, I hit him with a rage that he had not seen coming, having hardly registered the comment at all.

My insecurity about my looks and any other inadequacies had hijacked my better senses, moving me into a jealous rage. What fuelled my rage was a little protective voice in my head telling me all night that he still wanted something he couldn't have with me: breasts. It was protective in that it was protecting me from the threat of rejection, telling me to create distance to keep safe. In my mind, this part had turned a comment made in jest into an attack on my looks. It had made it all about beauty. As a result, I had blown things out of proportion and created a problem that, it seemed, in hindsight, didn't even exist.

My clients sometimes report similar responses. Whether they are out for a drink and a beautiful woman appears in the room or their partner has female colleagues or friends—or more recently, if their partner follows beautiful women on social media—the Beauty Load looms large, making them feel insecure and inadequate. The logic seems to go like this: our partner must see the other women and must see their beauty. Then here is the next leap that our fearful minds take … *therefore, my partner must want that 'beauty' more than he wants me.*

Fear of not being attractive enough takes over our better senses and our reality. This happened to me with my husband on this balmy evening in Sydney, despite us being loved-up newlyweds at the time. My husband would constantly tell me that he found me attractive and that my breasts were beautiful to him; and while I knew he was telling the truth, a deeper part of me clung to the fear.

His prior girlfriends all had, in my opinion, 'better' breasts. I reckoned—in my warped logic—that, as he had experienced something 'better', he must have been feeling the lack when he was with me.

After my jealous rage on that night, my husband did his best to reassure me. There was no part of him that wanted to be with his ex. There was no part of him that required more breasts than what my body offered him. He really did find me attractive.

It helped, but part of me still refused to believe him. There was a part of me that did not want to let his attraction register. It was as though I was so entrenched in my firm beliefs about my body that I wouldn't let go of them and let his attraction in. It was my protective part using this story of lack to keep me safe; to stop me from getting too comfortable and deeply immersed in this love in case I lost it.

At the time, it did not feel like I was doing this for safety.

All I could feel was anger. My deeper terror was masked by a ferocious projection onto him and all the ways that he was not making me feel good.

Rather than protecting us or delivering us the reassurance we seek, our fear often has the effect of disconnection. Projecting the fear onto our partners makes them confused and defensive, and this drives a wedge between us that stops us from getting closer, deeper and feeling more intimate with them.

It can feel like a risk to believe that we are attractive. Even though our fear does not make us happy or help us radiate our true beauty, it can be convincing.

We believe that our partner is making us feel a certain way, which is true to an extent; it is the partner (and in this case, the beautiful women too) who is pushing our buttons. But the buttons (those insecurities, the sense of lack, the sensitivities) are ours. Our partner is exposing in us the places that are sensitive and raw. It is painful, but it is also an opportunity to see ourselves more clearly. When we project this back on our partner, we do not get more intimate with ourselves and the parts of us that need our attention. Instead, we are running from discomfort again.

In my own married way, I was still avoiding discomfort, just as I had when I ran away from my date. But this time, I was not leaving my marriage or my man. I was using my discomfort around the Beauty Load to create distance in my relationship from the terrifying place of intimacy.

Chapter 18

We lose ourselves

Just before my husband and I got married, I lost myself by morphing into him. It happened so gradually that I was barely aware of it, that was, until I got an unpleasant wake-up slap to the face. The Beauty Load had got me so focussed on what my husband wanted and found attractive that I nearly lost me.

It was a Saturday morning in 1999, a few months before we were to get married. I was sitting on the edge of a football pitch, ready to go on and play. Playing football was part of this 'new me' I had created.

To tell this tale, though, I have to go back to a few months earlier when I walked into a hair salon and, due to the hot weather, told the hairdresser to 'just cut it all off.' I had not meant for her to take me so literally, but here we were, just months before my wedding, with not much more than a few millimetres left on my head.

So, as I sat on the grass on this sunny Saturday morning, I did not have my lovely locks. Instead, I had footy boots, shin pads, baggy shorts, a numbered strip and a near-bald head.

A young boy was sitting on the sideline too. He was looking at me oddly. To cover the awkward moment, I spoke to him. I can't remember exactly what I said to him. It is his response, not my question, that is etched on my memory.

He looked at me even more oddly, before turning to his mum

and saying, 'Mummy, that man just spoke to me.'

My heart fell.

I looked, apparently, just like a man.

How had this happened?

The conversion into being a carbon copy of my husband-to-be had been so subtle that I hadn't even realised it. Come to think of it, I *had* taken to wearing an item of clothing that, to this day, I still think is the ugliest thing on the planet—nylon sports trackpants. But that wasn't all.

Here was a snapshot of my partner's influence that I had taken on:

- I was playing football; he loved football.
- I had extremely short hair; he was bald.
- I wore the aforementioned ugly trackpants; he lived in them.
- I was eating man-sized portions for dinner. (He had the speediest metabolism in the West—I did not!)
- I was not wearing dresses or jewellery anymore; my feminine flow was buried deep.

In short, I was morphing into a genderless clone of my husband … which would be fine if that were a true reflection of me, but it was not. I loved him so much that I just wanted to feel safe. I wanted to feel that he loved me to such a degree that I had lost faith in who I was and was, it seemed, willing to replicate him.

Of course, I was going about this relationship all the wrong way.

What I was turning into wasn't a real version of me, nor was being like him the best thing for our marriage or attraction to each other. My husband—while he had a healthy dose of self-love—was not actually attracted to the reflection he saw in the mirror. He wanted me and the different energy that I offered him.

The wake-up call at the side of the footy pitch made me take a step back from the transformation and start on a trajectory back to a more real version of myself.

Yet, this wasn't the first time that I had become attached to a different version of me.

When we were first going out, I had an addiction to eyeliner. With blue eyes but very pale lashes, my eyeliner drew attention to what I believed was one of my best assets. The problem was that I was finding it really hard (impossible) to go anywhere without wearing it. I just didn't feel confident without it.

I suppose wearing eyeliner gave me a similar kind of confidence boost to what I got from the tissue tit trick. The difference was, most likely, barely noticeable by others yet made me feel like my appearance had moved from plain and unacceptable to something that I felt made me fit in.

While I was doing this for my man, it was he who shook me out of this compulsion. He told me that he preferred me in my natural state anyway. It was a struggle, but I managed to step away from the kohl pencil as an obsession and save it for nights out.

Laura Mulvey, whose theory of the male gaze we touched on in Chapter 3, delves into the concept in her 1975 essay 'Visual Pleasure and Narrative Cinema'. The theory suggests that women are portrayed in films and the media as sexual objects for the viewing pleasure of heterosexual males. Once you are aware of this idea, you see it everywhere. Women's bodies being presented in ways that please the male sexual norms and power structures. The male gaze has the woman as the supporting role to the hero. Sure, men's bodies are often portrayed in sexualised ways for the female gaze, but not on the same scale. Men are more often portrayed in ways that appreciate their skills, intellect or power.

There is a very obvious gap and we women can play into it.

There is a phenomenon I have heard about that has women all over the world getting up earlier than their husbands so that they can do their make-up before he wakes up.[57] Some women feel so self-conscious about the way they look naturally that they feel the need to put on this make-up mask at all times, even when spending time within their most intimate loving relationships and the privacy of their own bedrooms. These women are so invested in being pleasing to the gaze of their husbands that they sacrifice their sleep. I wonder, if they asked their husbands if it was necessary for them to do this, whether, like mine, their husbands wouldn't think so.

We want to change our appearance, but we also hold back other parts of ourselves.

What about the parts of us that we hold back because they feel too sensitive to reveal? What about the conversations that we don't have because we don't think our partner will react well? What about the sexual things we desire to explore but bury forever because we fear they don't match the image of the 'wholesome' woman that we aspire to be?

Deep down, we start to believe that we are safer hiding behind this tamer, more acceptable version of ourselves. We tell ourselves that it is this version and not our true selves that makes us worthy of love. The more we hide, the more we rely on the false version for our security and worth.

The problem with the question of beauty is that we are encouraged from an early age to put on these masks and hide parts of us away. We are encouraged to prune, mould, cover, enhance and extend. Little girls grow up watching their mums remove the hair from their armpits and legs, put make-up on, and shapeshift with push-up bras, high heels and big hair.

It is just what women do, right?

Chapter 19

We become sexually awkward

Years back, when a new suitor that I had lured into my embrace reached for my breasts, it did not have the arousing effect that you see in sexy movie scenes. After years of angst about this body part, telling myself stories on repeat that these breasts were making me unattractive, my response to a suitor reaching there was my body stiffening. My system would be on high alert and my thoughts would take over, critical, self-conscious and worried *What if my breasts are a disappointment?*

Breasts are more commonly an erogenous zone, a part of the female body that can signal the sensual and sexual self into readiness. But not for me.

HOW WE THINK ABOUT OUR BODIES AFFECTS OUR SEXUALITY

Being touched in the places on your body where you are most self-conscious can be awkward.

PAUSE FOR A MOMENT AND REFLECT

Do you have a place that is cringey for you? A place that you don't feel comfortable, confident, beautiful enough: your thighs, stretch-marked belly, cellulite arms or pimply back?

Your kneejerk response in intimate moments may be to karate chop your lover's hand away to save you from what your mind tells you will be *instant and guaranteed rejection* when they discover your flaws. I don't tend to use the karate-chop technique for fear that it wouldn't be very sexy, but it can, in those moments, feel almost impossible to sink into the appreciation of his hands on that part of my body and just go with the pleasure it brings.

If I am too entrenched in my head and my mind is filled with all that is negative about me and my body, I don't feel sexy. Even now when my husband reaches out for intimacy, if I am self-conscious, feeling negative about my body or in a head-led state, it can seem like there is a big gaping abyss of numbness standing in the way of me saying yes.

It is hard to be intimate when you feel self-conscious or are in the headspace of lack or shame. This can make it nearly impossible to connect intimately to yourself, your body or a partner. You can go through the motions and be physically present, but if you are not really there, you can't truly feel your body or the pleasure available to you. Would you agree?

A friend of mine has recently started dating again. This time around, however, being a mum of two, she is not sure how to feel good about her post-baby body. She wonders how she can feel comfortable exposing stretch marks, saggy breasts and a less-than-taut abdomen to her new lover.

Instead of relaxing into intimacy, our minds, in these moments, are dancing with thoughts, stories and presumptions. Stories that do not excite us into a yes for sex, but instead put the brakes on and get us stuck in our heads and stories about all the reasons we are not interested.

Stories such as:
- How can he even find me attractive with this [insert perceived flaw]?
- I can't even feel my body, let alone feel turned on.
- He hasn't touched me all day. Does he just want me for sex?
- I am so exhausted and tapped out. I just want to be on my own.

All this mental noise is a long, long way away from the feelings, the body, the senses, sensuality and above all, our sexiness. If we are stuck in our heads, quite frankly, we are locked out of our bodies.

PAUSE FOR A MOMENT AND REFLECT

What are the stories and presumptions that can
get you stuck in your head around sex?

HOW DID WE GET SO DISCONNECTED?

I don't know about you, but my sexual life started awkwardly. As a teen, it felt like I waited for years for my body to show me that I was a woman. I waited and waited so patiently, yet it just 'let me down'. Around me, other girls were turning into women, transforming from young things into *hot* young things, their breasts signalling their readiness for *more* in life. They were walking over the threshold from girls into sexual beings and the boys' attention was palpable.

My body, while it showed me all the other signs of womanhood, never came to the breast initiation party. I was flat-chested all the way through high school. Yearning, wanting my body to take the lead so that I could follow, I was far too embarrassed and self-conscious to guide my own way into womanhood.

This left me with an awkward feeling about being a sexual woman. It felt like I was a fraud, like I didn't really belong there. Due to cultural conditioning, I held the deep, warped idea that it was shameful to be sexual, and this made me feel like my body was keeping me perpetually at the age of twelve and that sexuality was just wrong.

Our insecurities about our flaws—aka the Beauty Load— have us feeling awkward about our bodies, which makes us awkward in our sexuality. This has two results. One: we get stuck in our heads, worrying about whether we are pretty enough or sexy enough, and thus we become less in touch with our sensual, sexual urges. Two: we lose our sense of entitlement to pleasure, boundaries and power.

Author Sonya Renee Taylor tells a story of a friend of hers with cerebral palsy. The friend was lamenting that she might be pregnant. Sonya, having been a sexual health consultant for many years, asked why she hadn't used a condom when she had had sex. The friend explained that having sex was already awkward enough with cerebral palsy as the positions were limited. The friend did not feel she had had the bargaining power to ask him to put on a condom—feeling like sex was already burdensome, feeling like she was lucky to have this man's attention, and not wanting to demand anything else and risk losing it. This moment of honesty struck Sonya and inspired her to utter the words 'Your body is not an apology,' which became the title of her book.

Hearing this story hit me with a recognition power punch in the guts. I know this feeling too. All those times that I put up with poor behaviour, disrespect and a lack of integrity and said nothing because I didn't want to risk losing whatever connection was available to me. These moments also stick out to me as the moments that I need to heal from and forgive myself for the most, even years later. They feel like a betrayal of Self, because they were.

I am worthy of decent behaviour, respect and integrity—we all are. I am worth losing a shitty connection to stand up for my needs and rights and I am always, always better off when I do so.

PAUSE FOR A MOMENT AND REFLECT
Do you know the feeling of not asking for the
behaviour or treatment you deserve?
What were the stories of 'not good enough'
behind this for you?

When it comes to our bodies and sex, it feels like there are layers of shame doubled over on themselves. Where does shame about how we look end and shame about being a sexual woman start? It is hard to extract the two from each other.

Shame seems to be an overarching feeling when it comes to women and sex, which does not help many of us relax and soften into the sexual moment, despite softening being so important to our presence and enjoyment.

SHAME MAKES SEX, INTIMACY AND CONNECTION REALLY AWKWARD

Sometimes shame just makes us feel uncomfortable and icky. Sometimes we escape these feelings in some not-so-healthy ways:

- Projecting the discomfort onto our partner in the form

of anger or blame, such as, 'You're not touching me in the right way!'

- Making excuses for why we won't be partaking in intimacy, like the old classic, 'Not tonight, honey. I have a headache.'
- Or just having disconnected sex, feeling numb and half-heartedly making the right noises.

PAUSE FOR A MOMENT AND REFLECT

How have you escaped the shame and discomfort of intimacy?

If sex is so wrought with feelings of awkwardness and shame, is it any wonder that as many as seventy per cent of middle-aged Australian women are struggling with low desire?[58] Why would we launch ourselves into an activity that brings up so much discomfort? But—and here is another contradiction of the Beauty Load—that doesn't mean we don't want it or that we don't want to be sexually attractive to others.

IF YOU WANT ME, THEN I MUST BE ATTRACTIVE

Despite those statistics and all the stereotypes that women are the ones who struggle with a waning libido and men are the ones who always want more, I have a lot of clients struggling with their male partner's low libido. This quandary seems to have a devastating effect on the female partner.

The problem is that women often attribute their partner's lack of libido to their own lack of attractiveness. 'He doesn't find me attractive,' they tell me. 'I mustn't be pretty enough!' they torturously insist. The same conclusion is very often reached when their partner has an affair. Our partner not wanting sex with us seems to hit us slap-bang in the body image sector of our self-esteem.

In an instant, these clients seem to overlook their partner's own mental, emotional or sexual issues and all other complexities in the relationship dynamics between them. The Beauty Load rears its head again.

Not being wanted by our lovers in general makes us women doubt our worth and lovability. We want to know that we can waft our sexual spell on the object of our attention, even if we don't choose to use it. The Beauty Load has us believe that it is our power to do this that makes us worthy.

PAUSE FOR A MOMENT AND REFLECT
How have you projected your beauty insecurity
onto your lover's experiences?

FROM MY NETWORK

How does the way you look affect your libido?

- 'When I'm overweight and not exercising, I definitely don't feel like sex as much.'
- 'When I feel very unattractive, I do not feel sexy.'
- 'If I feel fat, I just want to be alone.'
- 'When I feel pretty, I have a higher libido.'
- 'If I'm worried about a pimple or my skin, I won't want to have sex or I'll avoid situations where I might have sex.'
- 'If I feel yucky, I am less likely to want sex.'
- 'If I feel unattractive, I don't want to be looked at, let

alone touched.'

- 'Sometimes I think that he doesn't want to see me nude.'
- 'I think my boobs are gross after children.'

Chapter 20

We think sex requires beauty

Is beauty sex? Is sex beauty?

Beauty has been packaged up and sold to us as sexiness. But really, are the two as interconnected as we are made to believe? Your partner might get aroused by their perception of you as beautiful, but your sexiness is so much more than that.

In my personal exposure to mainstream porn, I am yet to see a woman who—despite having the neat, 'perfect' body and doing all of the sexy-looking moves and noises—actually looks like she is enjoying it.

What the porn and advertising industries do know and have packaged up for us is that good, satisfying sex needs its participants to be open.

Signs of openness embraced by the advertising and porn industries include:

- A slightly open mouth
- Youthful vigour
- A tongue licking the lips
- A neck slightly arched back
- A moan or a groan leaving the lips
- An openness in the face and eyes that says, 'Please take me, I will do anything you want'

And we see this everywhere. After consciously or unconsciously consuming this imagery for decades, we know the imagery of sex and sexiness. We know what to aspire to, if indeed we wanted to 'aspire'.

Here's the problem with that, though. You can't fake open. It is not about how it looks. To open means to be relaxed and heading towards pleasure. To judge whether sex is open or not is to go beyond the way it looks.

Bad sex is not open. It might be stiff and tense. Perhaps the participants are in their heads, worried, focussed on the result, brainwashed by porn or preoccupied with how they look … (hello, Beauty Load!) Open sex is more likely to be enjoyable for all participants. They will be tuned in to the moment and what brings pleasure for themselves and the other, and they will follow that pleasure thread.

PAUSE FOR A MOMENT AND REFLECT
How would you describe bad sex?
How would you describe good sex?

Nowhere in that description of enjoyable, open sex is there anything about having pert boobs, zero flab or cellulite, being young, or having a symmetrical vulva, but these are the things that often make us feel insecure sexually. Why? Well, these are ideals that the porn and advertising industries have made us believe matter in our quest for sexual attraction and satisfaction.

The problem with being exposed to sex through images, messages and media is that sex has been sold to us as beauty. Sex becomes all about how we look. How we look becomes the 'how to' of sex. But then what?

A 2008 BBC TV series, *Tribal Wives*, took frustrated British housewives and put them into different ethnic tribes all over the world for a month. The idea was to see how the women coped with the tribe and how the tribe responded to the Western woman. In one episode, a woman was placed in a tribe in which the women did not cover their breasts. The British woman was expected to show her breasts too but, just like many of us would be, was uncomfortable with the idea. The tribal women were confused. 'Why are your breasts any different to your hand?' they asked. 'It is just a part of your body.'

In Western cultures, our breasts are not just a part of our body; they are sexual objects. We have been conditioned to see breasts as objects with the power to provoke desire. By the time we are of these housewives' age, our breasts would have probably been personally sexualised in many ways by others; gawped at, commented on and fondled. We would have seen other women's breasts using their desire-provoking magic in the media and we ourselves might have played into this sexualisation with our own breasts, at times covering up to avoid a response and at others enhancing their sexual power and showing them off.

DOES OBJECTIFYING OUR BODIES MAKE US FEEL SEXY?

Dr Holly Richmond, a specialist in recovery from sexual trauma, shared the idea that young men have sex for pleasure and young women have sex for power. That hit a nerve of truth for me. My understanding of it is that in our early sexual life, as we head towards moments of intimacy, the guys might be thinking, *Oh yes, this is going to be so pleasurable, I can't wait!* while the young women might be thinking, *This person desires me—that means I am attractive and that means I have value.* And this, rather than pleasure, for the woman, is what feels powerful and satisfying.

PAUSE FOR A MOMENT AND REFLECT
Can you relate to sex being about power?
What are the conditions that help sex become
about pleasure for you?

As women, our ideas about what makes us sexy have become, to varying degrees, reflections on how the male gaze perceives us. Sex and sexiness have become less about how we feel or what turns us on, and more about how attractive and therefore valuable we are for those who are making love (or wanting to make love) to us. As such, we have become disconnected from how it feels for us in our bodies and become more focussed on how it feels for our partner.

Women are getting breast implants and plastic surgery on their labia not for their own sexual pleasure, because the surgery will, quite possibly, numb these parts down, dulling the pleasure at best, and causing pain at worst.[59] Conclusion? Women are not having surgery to feel more pleasure or arousal in sex for themselves but for the power they have over another's gaze.

While feeling that another desires us is a healthy and normal aspect of libido, it has become distorted in importance. The more our sexuality is about our lovers' experience, the more disconnected we are from how it feels for us. In focussing on them, we turn our gaze back into the critical authority figure ready to judge our performance and find fault, in this case the authority of our partner. Sex then becomes performative. Desirability becomes our aim, and how we are perceived is the priority, which makes us self-conscious and feeds our insecurity. The more we are focussed on them, the more we lose our connection to how *we* feel, what *we* desire and what turns *us* on. The less we soften and open to the present, the less we enjoy sex.

But also, the less we are tuned in to our bodies, the less we know what we like. We become more prone to getting less of what we want, forcing, faking and diminishing our own desires as a way of staying safe in our connection with our lover. You can see how not knowing what we want, wanting to be chosen and not wanting to interrupt the opportunity to be valued can cascade into dangerous predicaments for women.

The disconnection of women from their own sexuality starts young. From cultural ideas that women need to be virginal and pure to the notion of sex being 'wrong' and 'dirty', society tends to build brick walls between girls and the natural exploration of their bodies, their pleasure and their own sexuality. This can steer girls' sex exploration towards learning from an exposure to images, their peers' expectations and online visual clips and away from their own felt experience.

The Beauty Load has us focus outside of ourselves, seeking our satisfaction in the way our bodies look and are perceived by others, which means we are not tuned in enough to the way we feel.

I know this firsthand. If I am focussed on how my body looks, I am often critical, telling myself that my body is flat chested, bloated, pockmarked and unattractive. In this mind state, the idea of having my partner touch me seems hugely undesirable.

When it comes to sex, the porn and advertising industries have got one thing right: openness is the aim. Open to pleasure, open to our partner, open to the present. We want that, but, with all the noise in our heads, it is not always what we are able to achieve. When we have been conditioned to feel wrong, guilty, self-conscious and ashamed in our sexuality, the pressure to be 'open' can have the opposite effect. The more we think, judge ourselves and apply pressure, the more we are locked out of our inner experience in our body.

Personally, I am more open and ready to be intimate when I feel most grounded in my body, rather than judgemental of it. It is again a matter of getting out of the external authoritarian viewpoint voice and back into the voice of our hearts.

PAUSE FOR A MOMENT AND REFLECT

When do you feel more open and ready to be intimate?

We need to reclaim our sexuality for ourselves. More specifically, for our pleasure. Our bodies would not be wired with eight thousand nerve endings to our clitoris (double the number in a man's penis) if pleasure wasn't a worthy aim.[60]

Just like we become performative in sex and lose connection to our pleasure, the Beauty Load makes us become performative in life. When we are constantly viewing ourselves as if from external eyes, constantly taking selfies, looking in the mirror to know ourselves, being critical and judgemental of our bodies, we lose touch with our Self. Constantly imagining ourselves by the way we look and the influence our appearance has on others makes our whole lives performative. In being performative in life we lose our Selves; our connection to our feelings, our internal knowing and our values.

The Beauty Load makes us feel like we are not enough; not attractive enough, not good enough and not sexy enough. It has its sticky influential fingers entwined deep into our self-belief and the most intimate, private moments we share with our lovers.

I don't know about you, but I don't want to live like this. We want to reclaim our confidence, our bodies and our pleasure. So what can we do?

In Part III, I will take you through some practical and inspiring ideas to help us get out from under the Load.

Part III

How do we get out from underneath the Beauty Load?

TRANSFORMING THE LOAD

I sit here writing this chapter while on holiday with my kids, husband and some of my oldest and dearest friends. We are in a house just a two-minute walk away from a boardwalk that passes through mangroves and takes us to the beach. It is a holiday away from our daily routine, away from work, away from chores. And I can feel that it is also a holiday away from the Beauty Load.

Each morning, I have been chucking on some yoga pants and heading barefoot down to the beach with my dog, Coco. I revel in her joy as she runs, splashes, and chases the other dogs through the waves. I come back to the house for a hearty breakfast before we all head back down to the beach for a swim.

It is not Byron Bay with its uber-boho-chic Instagram babes or Bondi Beach with its young, hip, hot masses. It is a low-key kind of place, filled with families, retirees and people going about their business.

I am not taking many photos. I am not looking in the mirror apart from a glance here or there. I am not brushing my hair. I am not needing to dress for any occasion apart from diving into the ocean.

The friends we are with have been in my life for over two decades. They have loved and appreciated me through my twenties, thirties and now forties. They see me. The real me, beyond my looks, beyond my clothes.

It feels light, relaxing and liberating. I feel free to be me. I feel beautiful, by which I mean relaxed, confident, and comfortable in my body. Being beyond the Beauty Load like this feels so good. But how do we get this to stick in our normal everyday lives?

Culture doesn't change overnight, so the Beauty Load is not going anywhere. It is not going to evaporate off our shoulders of its own accord. If we want to live a life of confidence, self-acceptance and liberation, and of a kinder inner voice, we have to get ourselves out from under the Load.

In the next few chapters, I will look at the ingredients for getting beyond the negativity. What can we do to feel less of a load from cultural beauty expectations?

FROM MY COMMUNITY

What do you wish for in terms of beauty?

- 'That the botox and lip/face filler craziness would stop. I worry that this is becoming the new normal. I worry for my daughter.'
- 'To feel comfortable with myself.'
- 'No wrinkles or grey hair.'
- 'Less weight in problem areas.'
- 'No more facial breakouts, no more fat.'
- 'I wish to change a few things about my face. I wish to have skinnier legs and better tone in my thighs (I think about this daily). I want to feel confident in my skinny jeans and not cover myself up and [I want] the same in a bikini. I want to see what others say they see. I want to believe and feel pretty and no longer have any inhibitions.'
- 'To be seen as a beautiful person and BE beautiful to others.'
- 'That people didn't judge their worth based on their physical appearance.'

Chapter 21

Learning to feel beautiful

I rarely think about my breasts these days. They exist, they are part of me, there are pros and cons, but now I am not thinking too much about them. They just are. Maybe this is body neutrality. I have officially and eventually got over my disappointment and accepted the way they are.

What got me to this place is twofold. One: Recognising there was a problem with the way I was thinking and wrestling with it. Two: Getting permission to love and accept my body from other women.

RECOGNISING THERE WAS A PROBLEM WITH MY THINKING

I always presumed that the way I felt about my breasts would naturally change once I had breastfed my babies. I imagined myself falling completely in love with these impressive glands that could nourish life in such a connected and intimate way.

But in reality, after the breastfeeding was done, I felt even worse than I had to begin with. While I appreciated my breasts' efforts in feeding my young, I had also been given a taste of a voluptuous bosom, and the truth is, I mourned the loss. I had half-jokingly considered breastfeeding my children for years longer for vanity reasons, but it was not to be. Here I was, the other side of breastfeeding, with recently deflated breasts, still feeling loathe to accept them.

I desperately wanted to love them, because my aversion seemed somewhat juvenile and shamefully vain, but it was not that simple. I couldn't just *decide* to love them and be done with it. But still not being okay with my breasts after babies made me realise that I had a problem with the way I was approaching this. I was tired of hearing my own thoughts around them, I was tired of not feeling happy in a body that was clearly pretty amazing, I was tired of thinking about it at all. I wanted to get beyond this, which meant I needed to do some work on my thoughts and beliefs.

What I did and what I say we all need to do is get curious about our thinking and beliefs around our bodies, and to get more mindful.

Here's what has worked for me and some variations that have worked for my clients.

1. Challenging the thoughts

I started to notice and question my thoughts and the language I used around my breasts. When I tuned in to what was going on, I realised I was pretty negative about this part of my body. I was quite often saying or thinking things like, 'Flat as a pancake,' and 'What boobs?' or 'That won't suit me due to my flat chest.' Words have power. This had to stop.

I became conscious about the way I spoke of my breasts. Any time I noticed the dialogue was negative, I interrupted it, took a deep breath and switched my language to something more loving, such as 'That won't suit me as it is not the right cut,' 'My body is amazing' and 'I am enough.'

How do you speak to yourself about your body?
What are some loving or neutral replacements
for the negative thoughts you have?

2. Challenging the inner mean voice

Realising that my negative inner voice was trying to protect me really helped shift things for me. Just because you have a mean voice that tells you your body is not enough, does not mean what it says is true. It does not mean that you need to listen to it and follow it down the gnarly black hole into negative thinking. What it does mean is that a part of you is scared. That part really cares about you and doesn't want you to be hurt. Why does it worry? Because you matter to this part, because you are worthy of caring about. Why does it tell you horrible things, then? Because this is its way of keeping you safe. Telling you 'You suck—you are not pretty or beautiful or worthy' might save you from putting yourself out there in the world in a dating situation or thinking you are enough, only to be disappointed. This part tries to save you from that disappointment. It doesn't know the detrimental effects; it doesn't see the big picture, but that is not its job.

Your job is to remember that the part is scared. That its fear makes sense in this world and this culture, and that you don't have to follow the thoughts. We talk about how to calm this small scared part more in Chapter 22.

PAUSE FOR A MOMENT AND REFLECT

How does your small scared part make you feel?
How does it feel to think you don't have to follow it?

3. Reframing the problem

I reframed my thinking about my breasts' small size. To do this, I started looking for ways that I could be grateful for my breast size instead of disappointed by it. It turned out there was plenty to be thankful for about small breasts. For starters, they were not heavy, they did not hurt my back and I did not need to wear a bra if I didn't want to. Hell, I could even go for a jog without a bra on! I felt lucky that gravity was not unkind to my breasts post-kids.

PAUSE FOR A MOMENT AND REFLECT

What gratitude can you find for the parts of your
body that you feel negative about?

4. Getting focussed on my interests

At around the time that I was feeling ready to 'get over my boob issue', I became even more curious about the work I do in the world. I love reading, exploring, interviewing, counselling and being of service to people needing help in their relationships. It seemed the more I learnt, the more inspired I got and the more I wanted to learn. My focus on ideas, wisdom and collecting tools that might help others took up my focus and gave me so much energy that a shift happened. I no longer had time for thinking much about how people thought I looked. Also, I no longer cared quite so much.

Instead, I was thinking about the women who I truly admired, like Esther Perel, Grace Tame, Brené Brown, Yumi Stynes, Kasey Chambers, Turia Pitt, Emily Nagoski, Helen Mirren, Sarah Wilson and Sonya Renee Taylor: all women who are curious, brave, creative and focussed on their work in the world, not trying to fit a cookie-cutter version of beauty.

Show me a woman who is passionate and focussed on the work she does in the world, and I bet she is carrying less of a Beauty Load.

PAUSE FOR A MOMENT AND REFLECT
What are you curious about and why?

NB: If you can't work out your own personal area of interest, here are a couple of pointers. What section of the bookshop do you gravitate towards? What could you talk to your girlfriends about for hours? What would you do with your time even if you didn't get paid? Who are the women that you admire?

How could you step towards engaging in your interests a little bit more?

5. Realising that my happiness doesn't come from my external appearance

I noticed that the moments when I felt happy, relaxed, aligned, in flow and glowing from the inside … had actually nothing to do with the way I looked. In the moments when I felt beautiful, it was not from thinking about how I looked; it was more from being connected to my body, my heart, the people and world around me and the present moment.

I felt beautiful when I was oblivious to my looks rather than focussed on them. The moments when I thought my external appearance was all good, I may have felt confident, but the confidence felt unstable. I tended to be more in a state of comparison; there was a confidence, sure, but it felt like my bubble could burst at any moment.

Feeling beautiful is akin to confidence, which happens when I am relaxed and at ease. This, for me, means:

Space, rest, nature, play, giggles, deep connection with another, safety, great food, loved ones, delicious sensations, cool clear water to dive in, butterflies, flowers, the beauty of a sunset, the sensation of sun on my skin, seeing my children and loved ones in their elements, creativity, loving cuddles, great sex, tuning in to myself, feeling the divine.

PAUSE FOR A MOMENT AND REFLECT
Where does your happiness come from?

6. Focussing more on how my body felt than how it looked

As I have got older, I have become more and more tuned in to what works for this particular (and sensitive) body of mine and what doesn't. Whether that be food, drink, touch, intimacy, movement, physical therapy or healing. The more I notice this and respond according to what feels good and makes me feel alive, the more I feel my body and the more it feels good.

Our bodies are, after all, the valuable vessels that give us the opportunity to live life. When your body is in crisis and feels out of whack, sick or sore, your whole experience, your mental lens, the way you feel about everything is affected.

Your life is better when your body feels good.

For me, I try to offer my body what it needs by avoiding the substances that create illness, such as dairy products, gluten, caffeine (apart from my morning cuppa) and sugar (I told you I was sensitive!). I get lots of sleep and do exercise that is gentle, such as walking, swimming and yoga. I notice when I am running low on energy and offer my body rest. I allow pleasure and sensuality, whether it be savouring a delicious morsel, moving in a way that feels good or experiencing intimate pleasure. I create habits and boundaries that serve me and my energy.

Slowly, this shifts the value I recognise of my body from looking good to my health and wellbeing. When I focus on how my body feels and have gratitude for it and how it offers me wellness, I think and care less about how I look.

PAUSE FOR A MOMENT AND REFLECT
What makes your body feel healthy and alive?
What are you willing to offer your body to make
it feel even better? What are you grateful to your body for?

7. Clarifying my values

Focussing on how I looked and feeling inadequate as a result never really sat well with me. Even when my belief system was entrenched in the idea that I would never find love because of the way I looked, deep down a part of me knew that this was not really in alignment with my value system. I never wanted to be loved for my external appearance alone. I never wanted to be a trophy wife. I never wanted to be a model, praised for the lucky genetic placement of features. I only ever wanted to be loved and appreciated for me. That meant my heart, my ideas, my personality, my character, my passions and interests, and the quality of love and care that I offered those I loved. So why did I care so much about how I looked?

When I reassessed my values, my looks did not even register in the top ten. Even if they did, they would only be one of a variety of different values that I held, not the be-all-and-end-all of values to uphold (otherwise, as our scared part might have us believe, I should feel unworthy of love and attention!).

My top three values are connection, adventure and growth.

PAUSE FOR A MOMENT AND REFLECT
What are your top three values?

Here is a list of values for you to find inspiration from (remember, it is your definition of the value that counts):

Excitement, beauty, spirituality, growth, abundance, stability, honesty, adventure, integrity, learning, health, discipline, safety, friendship, respect, environment, harmony, love, creativity, independence, competence, fairness, happiness, order, philanthropy, compassion, accountability, gratitude, fulfilment, service, loyalty, leadership, cooperation, family, empowerment, freedom, community, change, ambition, tradition, responsibility, courage, authenticity, fun, flexibility and the way you look (better include that one too!) ... to name a few.

Why are your values important to you?

8. Finding joy in real beauty

Beauty is wonderful. As in the dictionary definition that I shared at the beginning of this book, beauty radiates joy and gives pleasure to those in its vicinity. Beauty is such an amazing part of life in fact, that when you think about it, you can find compassion for us as a culture/society/individuals for getting a bit obsessive about it. Getting unstuck from the Beauty Load does not mean that we need to stop finding pleasure in beauty— gosh no! Rather, it means that we need to stop defining beauty in such a limited way.

Think about how it feels to gaze upon something that you find deeply beautiful. For me, something that comes to mind is a beautiful tropical waterfall with a swimming hole beneath. What is it for you? Imagine it now. Close your eyes and pause for a moment; see this beauty in front of you and notice how you feel. Or even better, if you can, take yourself to a place that offers you real beauty in whatever form today and feast your senses. How do you feel?

These moments, if we allow them, fill us up with warmth, hope and the joy of being alive. They take us out of our minds, which become focussed on little troubles and problems; they bring us into the present moment and remind us that all is well.

Real beauty comes most often in the form of nature. It is the colours in the sky as the sun tucks itself behind the clouds, it is the tree growing courageously out of a crack in a rock, it is the colour of the ocean on a sparkly day, it is the glimmer in a friend's eyes when you share something with them, it is the playfulness of a puppy. The more we appreciate the beauty in nature, the more we start to appreciate the beauty in our natural state.

Real beauty in terms of the body is not limited to blonde, white, young and skinny. Sure, it is that (there is such beauty in youth), but it is also the curves, the patterns of cellulite, the array of colours and textures that skin can be, the change that a smile can bring to a face, the lines around the eyes that show a life well-loved or the bosom that comforts you in a much-needed hug.

When we remember that nature is real beauty, we see the real beauty in bodies as they are. And that, my dear, includes yours!

PAUSE FOR A MOMENT AND REFLECT
What would be on your list of things that
express real beauty?

Find something today that is real beauty. Take a moment to pause, breathe and enjoy the warmth it brings you.

9. Acceptance

Acceptance to me is about allowing space for imperfection and worthiness simultaneously. It is not either/or. Things don't have to be perfect. And if things are not perfect, it does not mean that they/you are unworthy.

Acceptance is knowing that your body (like you), while perfect in nature, is not 'perfect' in terms of the cultural ideals of beauty, that it has its flaws, and loving it anyway. It is cellulite, scars, small breasts, discoloured skin and love coexisting within you.

To find acceptance, we need maturity. It is not something we can get to easily as an adolescent when we still hold aspirations for ideals for our happiness. There is a level of internal stability and growth required to be able to trust that we are worthy of love even while imperfect. This maturity comes from grappling with our struggle, it comes from being with the discomfort and understanding where it comes from. This process is essential for our own sense of peace.

10. Getting help to get unstuck

Sometimes our mind becomes so tangled that even the best intentions and efforts can't seem to shift things or get to the healing we need. This is especially the case if you have experienced trauma or neglect in your life, or if the messaging is so repeated and prolific that things get entrenched (hello, Beauty Load!). What might be needed is a trained professional to help you share and untangle the factors that are keeping it stuck.

This certainly has worked for me. Therapy is an ongoing resource for me in my life whenever I feel stuck.

As a therapist myself, I love offering a safe place to allow clients to explore themselves and I love being held in this way by a trusted professional too.

After a time of consciously doing the work, I really started to feel a lot better. In fact, I was nearly ready to love these small breasts of mine.

GETTING PERMISSION FROM OTHER WOMEN

Issy was a woman who I guessed to be in her late fifties. She was the kind of older woman who I admired: alternative, worldly, open to growth, humble, and adventurous. On top of that, she had an eclectic style that made her agelessly cool. I was in awe of her effortless chic, but most of all, I was in awe of her unapologetic flat chest.

Issy was radiantly beautiful with her small breasts. She did not have a sniff of self-consciousness about her. She wore a tight t-shirt with no bra. As I watched on with my padding firmly in place, I thought she was beautiful. Being in her presence was like magic.

Issy appeared in my life at the moment I was ready to change my attitude to my boobs—all I needed from there was to be around her for a while, *et voilà*, I felt a deep internal sense of permission to love my own small breasts.

When I met Issy, I hadn't even realised that I needed permission to find my small breasts attractive. But I clearly did.

Seeing other women with our own kind of body, differences, race, colours or looks and seeing them unfazed, or better yet, claiming it as beauty, gives us permission to love and accept ourselves *even with this* point of difference.

This personal shift made me realise how important it is that we have exposure to body types that reflect our own. It is so important that our media reflects diversity and not something white and generic. In fact, it is so important that, where we can, we 'own' our beauty and stand up and be the role model for others. All you gangly, red-haired, freckle-faced, flat-chested young girls and women, look at me. *I own my body, I am beautiful and so are you.*

One of the great things about social media (although it can tear down all our confidence in a minute of scrolling) is that you can find whatever role model you are looking for easily. Social media can be a source of empowerment and belonging. It is important we choose our role models carefully, but there are plenty out there.

Some that I have found inspiring when it comes to the Beauty Load are the following:

- Kate Winslet now refuses to be touched up in her photos.[61]

- Taryn Brumfitt is the Australian author and speaker behind the Body Image Movement. Her film *Embrace* is truly inspiring.
- Sonya Renee Taylor is a leader, poet, activist and author of the aforementioned book *Your Body is Not an Apology*.
- Emily Nagoski is a sex educator and author of the brilliant and empowering *Come As You Are*, a book that explains that your sexuality is normal.
- Turia Pitt is the queen of self-confidence, teaching self-esteem and positivity to thousands. Turia had to learn how to walk, talk and live life again after suffering severe burns to sixty-five per cent of her body.
- Jameela Jamil is a body neutrality activist and host of the podcast *I Weigh*.
- Florence Given (@florencegiven) is a twenty-something queer feminist and the author of *Women Don't Owe You Pretty*.
- Thelma Plum, an Australian Indigenous singer/songwriter, has the songs 'Homecoming Queen' and 'Better in Blak', anthems that acknowledge the difficulty of being seen and respected as an Aboriginal woman growing up in Australia.
- Casey Donovan, an Australian Indigenous singer who recently hosted the SBS documentary *What does Australia really think about obesity?*
- Nakkiah Lui (@nakkiah), an Australian First Nations actress and screenwriter.
- Mia Mingus (@mia.mingus) is a disabled person's activist.
- iO Tillet Wright (@iolovesyou) is a transgender person's activist.

- Harnaam Kaur (@harnaamkaur) shares her journey with facial hair as a result of PCOS (polycystic ovary syndrome).
- Radhika Sanghani (@radhikasanghani) encourages people to embrace their profiles and shares her struggles with having a larger nose.
- Michelle Elman (@scarrednotscared) is a body confidence coach who had multiple surgeries and thus lots of scars to get comfortable with.
- April Hélène-Horton (@thebodzilla) is an Australian plus-sized model and body-love activist who refuses to let anyone tell her what to do, eat or think about herself.
- And I mustn't forget American rapper and songwriter Lizzo (@lizzobeeating), a label-shunning larger lady and all-round permission giver to be yourself.

Chapter 22

Getting comfortable with discomfort

A friend recently told me about seeing an ex at a bar.

'Did you say hello?' I asked.

'No way, it would have been too awkward!' she responded. 'I avoided them for the entire night instead.'

So, let's get this clear for a moment. Instead of saying hello, my friend decided to avoid all areas of the bar, all eye contact in her ex's direction and all trips to the bathroom that may have crossed his path. In trying to avoid awkward, the night, for my friend, became very awkward indeed.

Which is what we do, right? We avoid discomfort and awkwardness by going higher and further and doing more to manipulate, control and avoid. This might work for us when we are young and uncomplicated, with only one avoidance agenda item on our plates (i.e. one ex in the bar to avoid), but as we get older and our paths of avoidance get more and more complex and intertwined (i.e. multiple exes in the bar to avoid), we work ourselves into a small, confined space of existence. Ironically, in our attempts to avoid feeling awkward and uncomfortable, we get … awkward and uncomfortable.

WE DO THIS WITH THE BEAUTY LOAD TOO

I did it when I couldn't leave the house without eyeliner or was worried about being without my push-up bra. But I also did it when I had my push-up bra on and was fretting about being 'found out', or when I felt the need to shop for more clothes to feel okay about myself, drank myself into a groggy beauty confidence, ran away from suitors and morphed gradually into a clone of my husband.

These were all ways to avoid the awkward and uncomfortable feelings and thoughts that I was having about the way I looked.

THE SHOPPING, THE STYLING, THE PRUNING, THE SCULPTING … IS ALSO US AVOIDING THE DISCOMFORT OF IT ALL

The struggle to get comfortable with how we look makes us truly uncomfortable in the process, which is why I believe that we've got it wrong. We are approaching this as though the problem is that we are not beautiful enough. But the real problem with our fixation on beauty is that the Beauty Load makes us feel *uncomfortable* with our bodies, and the way we deal with that discomfort is all wrong. Realising that our looks aren't actually the problem is the bottom line of this book.

Why? Because when we realise our looks are not the problem, we take back our power. Instead of needing to listen to the cultural messaging—the media and the winks, nods and wolf-whistles from passing men—to see if we fit in, and then distorting ourselves into a small box of existence to feel okay, we just need to be willing to turn towards our discomfort and feel it.

Let's face it: as a whole, we are not great at dealing with

uncomfortable feelings. Most of us have never been taught what to do with them. Our culture has encouraged us to deny uncomfortable feelings and shove them away instead of acknowledging them or allowing them. Maybe it is not just the men and boys who are disconnected from their hearts, as we explored in Chapter 8.

In the moment of discomfort, it seems much easier to push the feelings down or distract ourselves from them, just like it felt easier for my friend to avoid her ex in the bar. In the case of the Beauty Load, this might look like turning to our external features and trying to 'fix' ourselves that way. We turn to all the bits of ourselves that don't fit the beauty agenda of the day, and we cover up, conceal, distract, remove, prune, tan, adorn … I'm guessing that you, like me, might feel better momentarily. But eventually the negativity seeps back up, and no matter how much effort we have put in, we still get a sense that we are not enough, followed by that inner voice getting all negative and hateful towards us.

The reason the negativity comes back is that the shoving down and fixing things on the surface does not make the discomfort disappear. Not at all. These actions are a bandaid giving us temporary relief at best from the uncomfortable feelings. Eventually, when we have this cycle of shoving away and then it coming back up on repeat, it only makes us feel worse. Not just because it makes us feel shit about ourselves, but also because the way we are responding is out of alignment with the love of our true Selves. It grates against that innate knowing that we spoke about as one of the contradictions of the Beauty Load, the part of us that knows we do not need to change to be enough.

For me personally, for so many years of my life, I was afraid of my uncomfortable feelings. They seemed so raw and unruly, so out of control. Control was the only thing keeping my life together (or so I thought), so my fear led me into a habit of denying, avoiding and shoving the feelings down. This seemed so much easier than trying to deal with them. But my system wasn't happy and let me know in the form of stress, chronic pain, migraines and depletion. It got to the point where my face was twitching … I couldn't hold it back anymore.

I HAD TO FEEL

At the time in my life when I realised I needed to let myself feel again, I also realised I no longer knew how. I was so out of practice that I couldn't even cry. I needed to cry, but first, I had to retrain myself in the art of feeling my feelings, which meant I had to stop ignoring them, for starters.

Ignoring or distracting ourselves from our feelings is like trying to ignore a kid telling you about a big problem; they will not go away. The child (aka the upset part of you) will keep trying to get your attention until they get you to listen. They will keep coming back, getting stronger and stronger in their delivery until they are whacking you over the head with a frypan to make you take notice.

All this 'crazy kid' upset part needs is to feel heard and understood. It wants what we all want, the most healing thing in the world; to be listened to and acknowledged.

When you turn towards this part of you and say, 'I'm listening. Tell me what it is that you are worried about,' finally, the upset part can hand over its burden of worry and relax a bit.

In the case of the Beauty Load, the frypan-wielding kid comes with messages of concern like:

- What if I am not (pretty, hot, beautiful) enough?

- How can I feel confident with the way that I look when everyone else is so put together?
- What if I am not lovable like this?
- Do I need to be different to be okay?

We are used to dismissing, shaming or minimising the distressed parts of ourselves. Generally, what we do is try to get rid of them as soon as possible. This is how we shove them down.

When we do something different, change comes. With our upset parts, instead of shoving them away, we can turn towards them with curiosity. We can accept that we have discomfort and allow whatever the upset part is feeling to be okay. When we do this, we start to create a sense of trust within ourselves, and over time, this is where our safety comes from.

Try this: Instead of pushing the upset part away, turn towards it, slow down and say, 'It is okay for you to be uncomfortable. It is understandable. I get it—the Beauty Load is big, heavy and stressful. I get that you are worried about me, and this is your way of keeping me safe. Thank you for protecting me, thank you for caring about me. How can I support you to feel less upset?'

This can often be enough for the frypan-wielding upset part to put down its weapon and exhale.

PAUSE FOR A MOMENT AND REFLECT

When you try accepting your discomfort,
what do you feel?

In looking after your upset parts, you become aligned with the central, essential part of you: your truth, which I call (inspired by IFS)[62] the Self. The Self is that loving part of you, the part that can offer care and nurturing. Rather than being overtaken by the voice of the small, scared part or the mean external authority figure, you can become the voice of love: the big Self inside you who has the capacity to love, accept and support all your upset parts. This is the part of you who has always known that you are actually enough.

The struggle of the Beauty Load is real. The discomfort is real. Let's stop running from the pain and offer ourselves some acknowledgement, acceptance and love.

Chapter 23

Attraction is more than beauty

A friend has recently gone through a break-up and it has made her feel ugly and fat. Her looks and her weight, I can guarantee you, have not changed, yet the way she feels and experiences her body has. Her mind has equated not being 'chosen' by this man with a lack of beauty. She is stuck in a perception of herself that comes from *If I were prettier and skinnier, he would love me.*

The Beauty Load has its tentacles deeply entwined with our self-confidence when it comes to love, dating and attraction.

BUT IS ATTRACTION ALL ABOUT LOOKS?

We meet someone new and we think, *Holy shit, this person is so hot!* We think they are beautiful and attractive. Then we get to know them, and our perceptions can go in one of these two different directions: either their beauty/attraction can blossom, or it can wane and disappear.

If we look into someone's eyes and they are sparkling, if they share their heart and we feel its goodness, if their values and thinking are in alignment with what we find important, then this person's beauty may blossom and bloom in front of our very eyes, no matter the surface configuration.

If, however, the pleasant looks are not backed up by decency, the aesthetics really don't have much staying power. If their behaviour is lacking integrity or you don't feel safe, what is beneath the surface won't appeal, and the way you see their looks will change instantly. The most beautiful human in the world's looks become superfluous and unappealing quickly if they reveal an ugly character.

AS WE ALL KNOW, ATTRACTION IS DEEPER THAN WHAT'S ON THE SURFACE

Even the subscribed to and agreed-upon ideals of 'perfect' beauty are not the keys to attraction. If they were, we would all find the same person attractive: the generic, cookie-cutter model types. What's more is they would be the only ones dating! But that's not how it works. These things are way more personal than that.

I am sure you have tried this: you go out to a bar with your friends and ask them to point out (subtly of course) who they find attractive. One friend might point out someone she sees and likes, but another friend will disagree and point out someone else. Chances are you all have *different* ideas about the physicality of attraction. Nobody can tell us what to find attractive, not trends, not gender, not fashions, not tick-box criteria.

Luckily for us, when it comes to finding a mate, attraction and beauty are more complex than what the advertising world and our pesky egoic thinking would have us believe. Good news! We don't all have to look like models to find love! We humans have complex physiology, biology and psychology at play. Attraction is a lot more personal, subtle and nuanced than is generally perceived.

Looks are a part of the attraction picture, of course, but is that part as important as we are making out?

LOOKS ARE RELATIVE

The way you see someone runs much deeper than their looks. Who you both are is central to attraction. Of course, there are people who *do* base their love on looks. Men who want the trophy wife, for example. Perhaps you have had an experience of this too? Maybe you've become fixated with a love interest purely on their looks. We know, though, don't we, perhaps from learning the hard way as I have (*I can't tell you how many times!*), that this is treacherous territory. What is more, these relationships can work, but generally because they have other things that are working in their favour. Because looks alone don't get us far in love. There is so much more to the equation of connection.

Here are some of the key elements of relationships that may be more important:

- Values
- Common interests
- Family culture
- Sexual compatibility
- Sexual chemistry
- Communication styles
- Ways of dealing with conflict
- Attachment styles
- Love languages
- Dreams for the future
- Willingness to grow together
- Mutuality of the commitment

If you were to put all these aspects of relationship in order of importance to you, where would beauty sit?

The truth of our attraction is deeper and more unconscious

than we realise. Let's explore some of the deeper aspects of intimate attraction.

OUR ATTRACTION IS OUR DESIRE TO HEAL CHILDHOOD WOUNDS

We are unconsciously drawn to a mate who displays the best and worst character traits of our childhood caregivers. Our subconscious has unfinished business, which means there's healing work to be done. Choosing a mate who exhibits similar patterns, behaviours and capacities to our primary caregivers (usually our parents) gives us an opportunity to revisit the past pain and heal. On a deep level, we want to grow and move towards better outcomes than we had when we were kids.[63] We see this partner as our opportunity for a more satisfying do-over.

On the surface, this may sound a bit far-fetched, but when you look a bit closer at your own relationship/s and the things that drive you crazy about your partner/s or really trigger you about them, isn't it generally the stuff that comes from your family of origin?

Perhaps part of the initial magnetic pull you felt towards your partner was subconsciously knowing that they would trigger similar stuff as your family. Now it just annoys you, but if you look at it a different way, could it be an invitation to heal some old emotional wounds?

OUR ATTRACTION IS BASED ON OUR SEXUAL POLARITY

We find our sexual energy match in a mate.

If we are in our feminine sexual energy, we will find someone in their masculine attractive and vice versa. If we are in our masculine sexual energy, we will be attracted to a more feminine energy. Those with balanced sexual energy will be attracted to others with balanced sexual energy.

This is sexual polarity and it is created by the difference between masculine and feminine energy. This is not about gender; masculine and feminine energy does not mean 'male' and 'female'.

Understanding this can help you understand why you are attracted to one type of person more than others.[64]

OUR ATTRACTION ENSURES GENETIC DIVERSITY

Pheromones are also a big part of our attraction to each other. You may not realise it in those initial moments of being drawn to a mate, but one of the things that is attracting you is scent.[65]

Biologically, pheromones do the job of ensuring that we don't end up with someone who is too genetically similar to ourselves. This is important because the continuation and evolution of our species depend on genetic diversity.

We are programmed to give off a scent that provides an indication of our genetic coding. Likewise, we are programmed to detect the genetic coding of another with the subtle powers of primal attraction. Humans are clever, aren't we?

ATTRACTION RELATES TO HEALTH AND REPRODUCTIVE ABILITY

Clear eyes; symmetrical face; red lips; rosy cheeks; certain proportions between hips, waist and bust—all the agreed-upon female beauty markers across the globe are actually signs of a healthy female individual. Across the cultures and throughout the ages, it is health and wellbeing that has been the one uniting force between the factors that we attach to beauty.

So, is all our worry about looking 'perfect' to attract a mate so necessary?

All this negativity and criticism that we focus on ourselves would imply that we feel we need to look 'perfect' to be worthy of attraction. This is why we come down so harshly when aspects of our appearance do not meet our standard. I wonder though, do we really want to look 'perfect'? Perfect in this case—meeting the ideals of the day—being the fashion, beauty and body shape expectations. Let's think about 'perfect' for a moment. Perfection is unattainable. I know that when I come across it, whether online or in real life, perfection tends to make me feel uncomfortable. It has the power to create within me a feeling of insecurity and the impulse to compare myself and feel less than as a result. Do I want to have that effect on others?

And what about our partners—do we want them to be 'perfect looking'? In the past, when I have dated someone who I perceived as extremely good looking, it has again filled me with insecurity and comparison. Comparison, in this case, to all the gorgeous-looking humans he could replace me with.

In fact, data from dating website *OkCupid* has shown that those with the most flawlessly beautiful profile pictures are less likely to find dates than those with less perfect ones.[66] I find my husband really attractive, but I don't want him to be a flawless beauty. Why then do my judgemental parts think that my partner wants flawless perfection in me?

The Beauty Load tells us that our looks magnetise our partner to us, and that we need to reach a certain standard to be attractive, but in obeying this idea, we really are missing the bigger picture. Attraction is all these more subtle and fundamental factors. When you strip it back to basics, attraction is our animal instincts—our innate need to confirm our genetic immortality.

For you to believe, as the Beauty Load may entice you to, that you are not attractive because you are not like the women plastered on billboards, and to opt out of self-worth and intimacy as a result, is a waste. I guarantee that the person who is attracted to you will find the combination of features and qualities that you have intoxicating in ways that you will definitely underestimate from that negative and nasty authority figure viewpoint.

In short, trust that you are attractive.

FROM MY COMMUNITY

What is your definition of beauty?

- 'Someone who consciously and wholeheartedly embraces all aspects of who they are—the flow-on confidence, peace, engagement and compassion (for self and others) as a result. Beauty, by this definition, is trustworthiness.'
- 'Someone with deep happiness.'
- 'Someone who is kind and has an authentic smile.'
- 'Someone who glows from the inside out but also someone who takes care of their physical attributes.'
- 'Someone who is confident in their own skin.'
- 'I believe everyone is beautiful in their own way. Beauty should be defined by the depths of your soul and the energy you reflect on others. Genuine, caring, kind to oneself and others, unconditionally loving and true is absolute beauty!'
- 'Radiance and happiness.'
- 'Someone who makes you feel good when you are in their company—heard, respected, accepted. Someone who embraces themselves just as they are and ages with grace (e.g. embraces the greys). A woman who stands in her feminine power.'
- 'Someone or something that captures your attention. It can be because of outside appearance or inner wisdom. Something that stirs a sensual (not necessarily sexual) experience within you.'

Chapter 24

Your beauty is inside you

Perhaps the most damaging impact of the Beauty Load is something even more subtle and self-perpetuating. The Beauty Load *keeps us* from being truly beautiful by having us focus on the surface of things. Instead of feeling good and radiating the good feeling, which could have the capacity to give pleasure, the Beauty Load makes us respond to our discomfort and lack with fear, looking for the next quick fix.

The world of consumerism has created a quick-fix culture, encouraging a kneejerk response to all our problems. Want to feel better? Take these pills. Want to look better? Buy this fake tan. Got an old model? Replace it with the new one. This goes for our health, our relationships, libido, mental health, happiness, and yes, our looks. 'Don't worry about looking at the causal lifestyle influences and bad habits that got you into this trouble,' the messaging soothes. 'Just get this and you can be fixed now.'

Yet, quick fixes are often dabbling on the surface in the realm of the transient. The surface, where we are scrambling around seeking our beauty, is not where our beauty is found. True beauty, as per the definition given at the beginning of the book, comes from depth.

So, let's go back to the definition of beauty we are talking about: 'the quality present in a thing or person that gives intense pleasure or deep satisfaction.' Where *pretty* is about the surface, *beauty* is not; beauty is a presence that can influence the heart. Beauty radiates out and touches the hearts of those in its presence. It's a radiance that comes from the development of character, an internal resilience, passion, acceptance of who we are, or an understanding that comes from grappling with a struggle, such as the one that the Beauty Load presents us.

In fact, facing the Beauty Load itself and processing it in a meaningful way brings us to a state of peace with our own definition of beauty. Grappling with the insecurity, the self-doubt, the sense of lack and the desire to make the quick fix are all standard rites of passage into our own inner comfort with ourselves. This very grappling can help us find wellness, acceptance and the capacity to be compassionate with ourselves. When we do this, we can live amongst the toxic air and pressure of the Beauty Load culture, and we can be present, compassionate and at peace with ourselves.

It is the grappling with and the depth that comes from it that makes us beautiful, as it takes us back into connection with our Self. It is the ownership of 'This is me, this is the way I look and this is okay.' This is what makes us beautiful. It is acceptance.

THERE ARE MANY WAYS TO BE HAPPY—PRETTINESS IS NOT A PREREQUISITE

You may know that even when you have the fake tan or have lost the kilos (or insert any other beauty goal here), you still don't necessarily feel a lasting sense of happiness.

PAUSE FOR A MOMENT AND REFLECT
Does the way you look impact your sense of happiness?
What are some of the things that give you a lasting
sense of happiness?

One way to gain happiness, and this sounds counterintuitive at first, is to stay present with ourselves and our problems. To know that we are willing to stay in the discomfort of doubt and get intimate with all the feelings that come at us gives us the satisfaction of knowing we can. It helps us trust our own reliability, strength and resilience, and enhances our sense of worth, as we have shown ourselves that we are willing to be uncomfortable in support of ourselves. We are worth that.

In every one of us, there is an internal battle being waged. A battle between the parts of us that just want to keep us safe (the small, scared parts) and the part of us that craves something deeper and more meaningful: an intimacy with life, with ourselves, with this moment and with another human.

In that struggle between our yearning to go deeper and the quest for safety, in which the *scared voice* booms loud, there is another voice—the voice of our Self. While our protective parts have us focussed on looking good in the world to stay safe, the Self knows we are enough already.

I can at times hear Self calling to me with a desire for more. Sometimes I respond and stay open; other times it feels too risky and I shut it right down.

If we only listen to the voice of the scared parts, we are kept in the shallows in safer territory. The fear has us turning away, distracting ourselves and trying to find that fictitious quick fix.

Even when I was young and running away from intimate moments, or addicted to eyeliner, or totally self-critical, my loving Self knew what was important and was calling to me, even as I ignored it. The Self always knows. If I ask it whether, truthfully, I need to look 'perfect' to be happy, worthy or loved, the answer would be no.

Do I want to hold love/life/experiences/myself at arm's length just in case I am not 'perfect'? No, I really don't!

My Self, just like yours, does not care for perfection or the way things look. They speak in the language of love—not looks, not veneer, not surface level. Your Self only ever asks, *Does this feel good/right/loving to you?*

In my formative years, my fear of intimacy made stepping into closeness with others feel like dangerous territory. My belief system of 'I am not attractive' did not match the attention I was receiving nor the action of stepping closer towards another, so I turned away. My terrified protective parts won the power struggle that was going on within.

In my relationship with my husband, my fear has, at times, been felt as insecurity and expressed as blame. At its root, this was me lacking trust in my own value. What it did in practical terms was hold me out of intimacy, one foot out the door to stay safe.

Does this resonate for you? Is there a longing deep within to explore something deeper?

If you feel that longing, here are five questions to initiate your own process beyond the surface. Grab your journal or find some space and sit with these questions, breathing deeply, staying present with yourself even if it is uncomfortable:

1. When did the belief 'I am not attractive' (or insert your own negative beauty belief here) first come into your awareness? What is this part of you afraid would happen if you did not hold on to this belief?

2. Do things need to 'look perfect' for you to feel happy? What brings you true happiness?

3. How are you grateful to the part of you that is protecting you by having you focus on fitting in?

4. Does your Self prefer to hold things at arm's length (in case they're not perfect) or experience/live/get intimate with life? Why?

5. What would be the first small step you could take to get more intimate with life?

Chapter 25

It comes and goes

Only a month or so ago, I had one of those phases where I just felt bad about the way I looked. Do you have those moments, those days, or those weeks, when every time you look in the mirror, you just feel really sad?

PAUSE FOR A MOMENT AND REFLECT
When did you last experience a phase of feeling
sad about your looks?
What was the focus of your attention?

For me, in this particular patch, my issue was aging. All I could see in my reflection was the sagging skin around my jawline, the wrinkles, the bags under my eyes and my blotchy face. It was like I had reached a new level of aging and I just couldn't help but focus in on it.

Even with all the work I have done on beauty, even while writing this book about not wanting to get stuck in an obsession about external expectations, even with all my strategies for transforming the Load ...

I still felt it.

A few days later, I felt better. I am now back to looking in the mirror and seeing my full self and not just the zoomed-in-on sagginess and flaws. But the point is, it sucked for a few days. And it will suck again in the future.

It is not like we are going to deal with the Beauty Load, get comfortable with our looks and be done with it, never to be bothered by niggling thoughts of body image again. No! Sadly, the culture of the Beauty Load will always be there as we pass through different phases and stages.

One thing that unites us all in the stress and pressure of the Beauty Load is aging. We will all lose our youthful looks to age and have to deal with the discomfort that that brings. Aging, in a world obsessed with a beauty defined by youth, is akin to becoming invisible. The older you get, the less you get noticed, appreciated, validated or even given opportunities. One of the first signs of aging that my friends and I noticed gave us mixed feelings: it was less harassment from random males. We didn't want it, but now that it is gone, it leaves us feeling invisible and in a strange way like we want it back.

We can't avoid the Load, but what we can do is be more aware of the toxic pressure and be more compassionate to ourselves about feeling it. Instead of getting critical and down on ourselves, we can instead let our inner upset part know that this is the Beauty Load and it is not personal; it is inevitable. As well as that, we could share our experiences of the Load with a trusted friend, find a subculture of acceptance and work with the tools that we have in our own personal toolboxes to manage the discomfort. Little by little, the weight of the Load gets easier to manage.

So, let me go first, knowing that you, my dear reader, are just like a trusted friend. I will share with you some thoughts that I still have regarding the way I look from time to time.

- My tummy is too flabby and loose.
- I need to lose weight.
- I wish I had bigger breasts.
- I have nothing to wear.
- My skin is wrinkly, saggy, and old looking. It's sad.
- Will my husband still find me attractive if I start looking too old?
- I wish I were fit and slim like [insert name of someone I have just seen who looks fit and slim].
- Will my ideas, thoughts and projects (such as this book) be valued if I am not young and hot looking?

PAUSE FOR A MOMENT AND REFLECT

What worried thoughts do you have about
your body/looks?

These thoughts come.

Prior to me realising there was such a thing as a Beauty Load, these thoughts worried me. I would follow them down a rabbit hole of worse thoughts and horrid fears and I would take them seriously. These thoughts would create a narrative about myself that was so negative. I would worry on them, allow them to make me feel sad and gross and insecure, and have all the fears that came up with them.

These days, I see these thoughts differently. I see them as a natural result of growing up in a culture with the Beauty Load. It is no longer relevant whether these thoughts are true, because everything is subjective, relative and comparative. Now I realise that these thoughts are much more about the culture and context that I have been conditioned in, than a reflection of me.

I also know that these thoughts come directly from my

protective parts. My parts are always looking out for me and wanting to keep me safe in their singular-minded way. It makes sense that my protective parts would consider looking good in the world as a way of keeping me safe. Of course, they want to keep me safe by having me try to fit in. My parts care about me and allowing the presence of these thoughts reminds me that they care, which feels helpful.

I know now that I do not have to worry about the fact that I have these thoughts. They do not signal that there is something wrong with me. They do not signal that I have to fix anything.

All I need to do is have compassion for my worried parts. When I turn towards them and say, 'Hey, I get it. I understand that you are scared and that this feels uncomfortable. It makes sense. How can I support you?' they tend to relax. Usually, my worried parts just need reassurance from the bigger, loving me, and a hug.

In short, it is normal and totally expected to cycle through the ups and downs of how you feel about your body. Just because you feel shitty about the way you look today does not mean that there is anything wrong with the way you look, nor does it mean that you will feel like that tomorrow or forever.

Chapter 26

A new culture

Whenever I say anything to my friends about feeling ugly or uncomfortable with my body, they respond exactly the way that I would if they had said the same thing to me. They tell me, 'But no, Nicole, you are beautiful.'

Which is sweet. They are trying to comfort me. They know that for me, feeling unattractive is uncomfortable, not because I am overly insecure or overly vain, but because the Beauty Load bears her weight down on us all and tells us that our beauty equates to our worth.

I am grateful that my friends jump in to try to ease my discomfort. I am also grateful that they validate my beauty. Yet, the satisfaction is short-lived, because in their attempts to comfort me, what they have done is denied the truth of my struggle.

When my friends respond to my struggle with 'But you are beautiful,' what I am hearing is:

- Don't be ridiculous
- You shouldn't feel that way
- Don't be blind to your blessings

And then it feels like they are saying that I am petty, silly and vain. And they may be right. I may be petty, silly and vain. Of course, there are millions of people with reason to struggle harder than me. Of course I should feel grateful for what I've been blessed with. I have a lovely, healthy, functioning body. *Geez, get over it.*

My friends, bless them, are really trying to make me feel better by jumping straight over my discomfort and getting down to the solution, which is my warped view of myself. They know that the solution lies in me getting over this view of myself and learning to see myself as beautiful.

And I could perhaps jump to that, but I have tried it and found it doesn't work. What happens is I only feel the enjoyment of my beauty and this Load-free zone for a moment before being thrust back into my dysmorphic filters. Not because it's not true, but because for one thing, I would have brushed my upset part aside without acknowledgement. But also, the culture and pressures and shame of the Beauty Load are always waiting, ready to load me up again as soon as I am not focussed on my new and improved self-view.

Being told that I am beautiful and 'shouldn't think otherwise' is, in short, not what I need. What I need from my lovely friends is for them to really get it. I need them to acknowledge that the Beauty Load is hard for me at this moment. I need them to see me in the struggle and offer the life raft of understanding.

I was talking about my need to be acknowledged in the Beauty Load with my friend Lisa. A short time later, Lisa was talking to another friend of hers. As they chatted, the friend shared that she was really struggling with her stomach flab. Lisa felt herself ready to launch into the usual 'comforting' script of 'But no, your tummy is fine, you are beautiful,' but stopped herself, remembering our conversation. 'I get it,' she said instead. 'I know exactly what you mean. It's the Beauty Load and it makes it hard to accept ourselves at times.' Her friend let out a sigh.

PAUSE FOR A MOMENT AND REFLECT
What do you need from your friends when you are
sharing your struggle with the Beauty Load?
How would it feel for your friends to respond to
you with understanding?

We live in a patriarchal, capitalist, consumerist society. One in which we are waging wars, destroying the planet, disrespecting the traditional owners of lands, putting power above decency, and worshipping the dollar above all else.

It is not all doom and gloom—there are amazing people doing incredible things; life rafts of hope, such as teen environmentalist Greta Thunberg and body image advocates like Taryn Brumfitt.

But the reality is: things still aren't great.

My question is this: do you want to put the trust in the way you feel about yourself in the hands of this culture?

Big business, social constructs and the media don't give a rat's arse about how you feel and nor do they feel they should. From their perspective, their job is to sell stuff and stay powerful, not look after how you feel. Allowing our culture to influence how we feel about ourselves is not healthy. In fact, it is a form of self-neglect. You wouldn't put your diet in the hands of mass culture, would you? If you did, you would probably be sluggish, addicted to salt and sugar, unhealthy and numb. Most of us will think about our body's needs when considering the diet that is best for us, despite the ads and availability of food. It's time we did the same with messages about body image.

What we choose to put in our mouth is like what we choose

to take in as a belief about ourselves. The shit stuff is out there, but we can choose not to consume it.

Yes, when it comes to beauty, the imagery makes us feel ugly, lacking and insecure. Yes, the messages do not make room for us and our particular reality. No, there does not seem to be a sense of acceptance for the exact version of beauty that we have. But that does not mean you need to swallow it all and hate your body. Instead, it means you need to be gentle, loving and fierce in the way you look after yourself and your particular version of beauty, just like you would with your particular dietary needs.

The Beauty Load affects our self-esteem, which is our measure of how we respect, love and value ourselves.

Self-esteem takes us to a choice point. We stand at a crossroads.

If we turn one way, we choose to please other people and compensate for our sense of not being enough by becoming what we think they want us to be. In order to do this, we need to tuck our needs away.

If we turn the other way, we choose our Selves and our own needs. We become the advocate for ourselves, we own it and we make the choice to respect our own boundaries (what feels right and what feels wrong for us), needs and desires.

When we feel that we are not enough, we make the choice to compensate and people please. We can only choose the path of our needs when we have enough self-esteem to see ourselves as valuable.

When we believe that our looks are what give us our worth and, because of the messages we are surrounded by, that our looks are not enough, then we become vulnerable. Our self-esteem becomes fragile. We feel the pull to find safety by choosing other people's preferences above our own. We start to believe that this is where safety exists, in pleasing others. We start to believe that we really are not worthy of having our own needs met. The more we people please and compensate, the less we even know who we are or what we want.

The habit of doing this over and over makes us lose ourselves more. It corrodes our belief in ourselves and our clarity about who we are and what we need to be okay. This, like any self-fuelling loop, can get us stuck so that people pleasing and compensating feels more and more like the only choice we have.

It is natural and normal for us to have gone down the first path of people pleasing at certain points in our lives, particularly in adolescence. It is normal to have become lost and then have to reclaim our boundaries and our needs when we find ourselves off track in the woods.

I recently got back from a holiday and did what many of us often do: I jumped on the scales. In doing so, I found out I had gained three kilograms.

My kneejerk response was pretty typical. It was firstly, 'Well, that's the sign of a good holiday!' Swiftly followed by, 'Well, I had better get to the gym and eat healthily to lose it, quick smart.'

But then I paused and thought, hang on a second, screw that! Why should I? I am not unhealthy, not unhappy, not even unfit.

My kneejerk response had me edging towards self-criticism and negativity for my new curves and rolls. I felt gross! But when I paused and sat with the feelings, I realised that feeling gross and negative was not my truth. It was my conditioning.

Feeling gross for being bigger was how I had been primed to feel by a society that is obsessed with women as small, voiceless objects of beauty who will spend their dollars if they feel gross. The preening and grooming to make us conform and make ourselves small is part of the sick obsession, the sick grossness that I was feeling.

This conditioning was not something I wanted, nor chose,

nor was it a culture that I trusted with my mental or emotional wellbeing. Who says I need to be skinny (skinnier) to love my body? Advertising, marketing, a patriarchal society and brainwashing. That just makes me angry; I never wanted to trust my values to them as my guidance system. I do not want them to be in charge of my self-esteem. *So why should I be guided in this now?* I wondered. *Why not choose to love this healthy body right now as it is? Why need it to be kilos lighter, slimmer or neater in order to find it acceptable?* I could find no reason.

My flesh is beautiful. My curves are sumptuous. I am happy, healthy, fit and for now wearing all my clothes that have elastic waists.

Remember the shame expert Mario Martinez, who I talked about in Chapter 10? He said that if we stray from the rules of a culture, we will be shamed. That sounds a bit depressing, right? Perhaps you are wondering if I'm suggesting that we stay trapped in the culture of the Beauty Load forever and strictly adhere to its strategies for fitting in.

No, I am not!

There is another way. Martinez also said that there is a way out without the damaging effects of inflammation and shame, which is to move to a subculture of support and alignment.

We can't do this alone.

But we can do this together.

If we create an accepting, supportive subculture beyond the Beauty Load, we can shed the oppressive weight of mainstream Beauty Load culture.

This is how I see our subculture working:

- We praise and support each other for our deeds, actions, values and creations, not just our looks.
- We look for, nurture and appreciate the deeper beauty in ourselves and others.
- We are passionate about lots of things that give our lives meaning and purpose.
- We acknowledge our own and our friends' struggles with the Beauty Load and allow space to wrestle with the discomfort.
- We are comfortable with things being uncomfortable and we trust that feelings, if we allow them to be felt, will change.
- We console and comfort our own protective parts who want us to be different to what we are, and we understand that this is an inevitable part of having grown up in a culture obsessed with looks.
- We shift our focus from how we imagine an external authority figure sees us to the eyes of love, and we start to feel and enjoy being alive in our own bodies, in this moment.
- We still enjoy the rituals of beauty and we do whatever we feel is necessary to feel beautiful without internal judgement.
- We adorn and preen and style ourselves lovingly so as to feel beautiful, rather than because we feel we have to to be acceptable.
- We support beauty diversity in the media. We vote with our dollars.
- We come up from shame and down from grandiosity to be face-to-face with being a messy human with the

rest of the messy humans in our lives.
- We celebrate beauty in nature and help heal the planet by reducing our consumption of beauty products and fast fashion.

Who are the people/groups in your life where the above subculture would be possible?
Who are the people/groups in your life where the above subculture would not be possible?

FROM MY NETWORK

What makes you a beautiful woman?

- 'My kindness, my smile, my great listening skills and calm nature.'
- 'How good I feel on the inside. My happiness and confidence.'
- 'Some days when I feel good and my hair has been done, I feel beautiful. I know my figure has always been reasonably good. When I feel excited and interested, I forget about me and just enjoy the moment.'
- 'I have a genuine love of animals. I love my children and would do anything for them. I'm cheery on the outside. I'm chubby but cute.'
- 'Lips and eyes, hair (although it's no longer natural) and my laugh.'
- 'My intelligence and my heart.'
- 'My energy and spirit.'
- 'That I am loving and laugh often, but this is not often seen at first glance. It is our outer packaging that often attracts others and [this] may be why it gets more emphasis than it should.'
- 'My personality, humour, kindness and toned physique.'
- 'I am me in my entirety. To some, I am beautiful. To others, I am plain. To others still, I may be ugly. I can tell you what physical features I like best, but I don't think that is what makes me beautiful. I think beauty is honesty. It is comfort in yourself, without ego or vanity.'

- 'My intelligence, my wit, my eyes, my hair, my unique features.'
- 'My big brown eyes, olive skin, happy nature [and] positive outlook. My breast size, [my] thick brown hair. My empathy and kindness to others. My sparkle and willingness to laugh as much as possible.'

Chapter 27

Your beauty

I don't know the words or the angle that will help minimise the Beauty Load for you. All I know is that I wish you didn't feel it. I wish that you felt enough, or even better, I wish you felt truly beautiful.

But I know it is hard.

Your struggles are and have been very real. It has been a tough road. The pressure is real. The pressure is not even a personal buy-in. It is way bigger than you. It is a huge deal, as massive as the culture itself.

Your discomfort makes sense. I get it.

Until we can acknowledge that this load we feel is the culture and is not about us personally, until we can forgive ourselves for how we are, how we work around our discomfort, how we react in defensiveness, how we indulge in the quick fixes and judgements, and do so in a loving way, nothing is going to change. We are messy humans, in a toxic world, doing our best. It's okay.

If you are reading this and feeling like your body has let you down, is not enough or takes a bit of work, or like you can only feel okay if you go to all these lengths, it is okay.

You are okay.

But the truth is that your body is not the problem. The way you have been conditioned to think about your body is the problem.

Your body is enough. Your body is yours. It is the only body you are going to get in this lifetime, and it is doing a pretty good job at allowing you to live life.

It is time for you to lay down your resistance and embrace what you have, because what you have is enough.

The question is not what is wrong, but what is right with your body.

Grab your journal and make a list of all the things that are right with the way your body:

- looks
- works
- feels
- grows
- nourishes
- enjoys
- senses beauty

Quite a lot is right with your body. Let's be done with being down on this beautiful body. Let's let go of needing it to be more or less than what it is. Let's release the external authority viewpoint or the need for validation from others. Let's practise looking at our bodies through the eyes of love.

The body that you have might not be other people's vision of perfect, but it is perfect. This is your perfect. Perfect for you to live your life.

We were all born different. Different in terms of shape, colour, texture, race, ability, health, hairiness, wealth, size, sensitivity, gender, etc. Whatever it is, it's okay.

Think about what you would want your sons and daughters (real or imagined) to think and believe about their bodies. I'm imagining that you would tell them something along the lines of, 'What you have is enough. It is you and you are beautiful.'

When you think about it, beauty is so much more than the airbrushed perfection that we have been brainwashed into thinking it is.

- Beauty is wellness
- Beauty is life force
- Beauty is ownership
- Beauty is love/compassion
- Beauty is strength and resilience
- Beauty is what emanates from your heart

Beauty is what shines through when you are in a state of ease. *We* are the role models for beauty—not the TV, not the ads, not Instagram. Let's not give big corporations or Insta models that power.

It is us and how we show our kids how *we* love *our* bodies that gives them permission to love theirs.

I have always loved Keats line that I share at the beginning of the book,

Beauty is truth, truth beauty, – that is all Ye know on earth, and all ye need to know.

To me this says that we find our beauty when we accept and are true to ourselves. It says that beauty is not in the covering, hiding or fixing, but in the loving it all. To me, this line says, own it. Step both feet in. Commit to accepting the truth of the way your body is. Not once you have the bikini body, once you have cleared up the pimples, or once you have lasered away every hair, but *right here and now!*

When you do this, you give us all permission to love who we are, even though we are not perfect either. You start to change the culture for the people around you. Little by little, this spreads until there are pockets everywhere of people claiming their beauty, and the culture of the Beauty Load starts to change.

When I see you accepting your body and your beauty even if (especially if) you don't fit the beauty ideals of the day, I feel like I can do the same. I feel empowered seeing you feel empowered. I have permission seeing you give yourself permission. I feel like accepting my body when I see you accepting yours. I can love me more when I see you loving you more. And when you see me doing all these things, you feel the same.

I know for me, I have always wanted the depth of love and beauty. To love myself for who I am.

I wanted to love me—the whole, full me that I could see, feel and sense: the Self. The part I could connect to through the windows of my eyes.

I always had a fleeting sense that I did love that me, but I could lose the fragile touch of it when I was uncomfortable with my reflection or caged in by my ego. Now it is time to stand firm in that love.

PAUSE FOR A MOMENT AND REFLECT

Have you wanted to love the deeper part of you too?
Do you feel ready to love the deeper part of you?
What do you love about you?

In a world that is obsessed with how you look and that encourages comparison and criticism, we can forget all the great things that we love about ourselves. Aside from your body, when the fear and doubt is not front and centre, what do you love about you?

Grab your journal and make a list of what you love about:
- the qualities you possess
- the things you love and hold dear
- the way you care

- who you are deep down
- how you show up in the world despite your fear

Maybe you love that you are: brave, creative, caring, wholesome, easygoing, full of love, thoughtful, sexy, kinky, faithful, daring, diverse, clever, colourful, wise, humble, out there, hopeful, generous, values driven, ambitious, careful, carefree, quiet, protective, sensitive, tuned in, open minded, kind … etc.

Now close your eyes, and breathe into the feeling of knowing what you love about yourself. Let yourself really feel it and appreciate this energy of who you are, of love. Perhaps this is a clue to who you are without the fear, stress and protection of the Beauty Load weighing you down.

Come back to this list and feel this love you have for yourself. Doing this practice again and again will help to build a solid sense of self-love.

PAUSE FOR A MOMENT AND REFLECT
Who are you without the Beauty Load?
How does it feel in your body?
What feels possible without the fear and doubt
of the Beauty Load?

DAILY COMPASSION DECLARATION

To finish, I want to leave you with a daily compassion declaration for you to repeat to your Self and your body.

With repetition, this compassion declaration will help gently shift the way you experience the Beauty Load and connect with your body. This exercise will work even more powerfully if you say it looking into your own eyes in the mirror.

Let's say it together out loud:

Even though it can sometimes feel hard,
I accept that I am enough.

I acknowledge the pressure of the Beauty Load and how difficult this journey has been for me. I acknowledge the pressure I feel every day to be beautiful and I see that it comes from the culture and my protective parts caring about me.

I forgive myself for thinking that this was not the kind of body I wanted it to be.
I am grateful for all that this body has taught and given me.

Little by little, I allow myself to accept my body, warts and all. Little by little, I let go of seeing myself through the external authoritarian mean-girl eyes.

I see myself and my body through the eyes of love.

I acknowledge the beauty that emanates from deep within me. I enjoy the feeling of being alive in this body.

I embrace all of me.
I am enough.

Acknowledgements

I wrote this book on Yugarabul, Yuggera, Jagera and Turrbal land. I acknowledge that sovereignty has never been ceded. I acknowledge the People who are the traditional custodians of this land. I pay respect to the Elders past, present and emerging. I am committed to honouring Aboriginal and Torres Strait Islander Peoples' wisdom, heritage, beliefs and continued connection to Country.

Thank you to Natasha from the kind press for just *getting* my message, and for treating it with such respect. Thank you also for being so easy and professional to work with. Thank you to both this book's editors: firstly Kris Emery for helping me to see the little glimmer of light that needed honing, and secondly Georgia for helping these words to really shine. Thank you to the cover designer, Mila, who nailed it. Also thanks to my original cover designer Justin Huehn, who did a wonderful job of bringing my original concept to life.

Thank you to all my writing guides for paving the way in such unique and powerful ways: Katie Dean, Kris Franken, Lauren White and Anne Moorhouse. I feel so much gratitude to you all.

Thank you to my cheerleaders near and far, of which there are so many. Special mention goes to my beloved Tripod; thank you Alana and Che for your constant loving acceptance and support in all the things. To Kimmy for supporting me and this book and putting aside a whole weekend (among other things) to nurture it forth. Thank you to Krissy for always cheering me on.

Thank you to my clients who had the courage to share their fear, their shame and their load with me. Holding space for the hard things that people share is the greatest honour of my human experience. Thank you also to the women in my network who courageously filled in a survey full of awkward and vulnerable questions, the responses of which are sprinkled throughout this book.

Thank you to Dick Schwartz, the developer of the therapeutic model IFS (Internal Family System), on which a lot of the ideas of Self and 'parts' threaded throughout this book are based. His model just kind of clicked with me and helped me make sense of the internal world.

Thank you to my parents and family for all the love and support and to my children for inspiring me to write about this issue and allowing me the time and space to pursue my passions.

And last, but not least, thank you to my husband for always finding me beautiful and reminding me to get over my negative stories and my EGO and trust that I am enough.

Sources and further reading

For recommended reading, a Beauty Load work sheet and a guided meditation, please visit **nicolemathieson.com/bookresources.**

Part I

1 Dictionary definition of beauty, date accessed 6/12/21, dictionary.com/browse/beauty

2 'Film Theory 101— Laura Mulvey: The Male Gaze Theory', date accessed 12/12/21, filminquiry.com/film-theory-basics-laura-mulvey-male-gaze-theory

3 'Social Comparison: An Unavoidable Upward or Downward Spiral', date accessed 6/12/21, positivepsychology.com/social-comparison

4 'Mia Freedman: "It's 2019 and I now feel bad about my eyelashes.", date accessed 6/12/21, mamamia.com.au/eyelash-extension-trend

5 'Eating Disorders—A Current Affair: An introduction' by the National Eating Disorder Collaboration (2012)

6 'Insights into the Concerns of Young Australians: Making sense of the numbers' by Mission Australia (2010)

7 'Sex differences in the relationships between body dissatisfaction, quality of life and psychological distress' by Scott Griffiths, Phillipa Hay, Deborah Mitchison, Jonathan M Mond, Siân A McLean, Bryan Rodgers, Robin Massey and Susan J Paxton (2016)

8 'Former Vogue Editor: The truth about size zero', date accessed 12/12/21, theguardian.com/fashion/2013/jul/05/vogue-truth-size-zero-kirstie-clements

9 'Entrapped by the Beauty Industry: Eating and body attitudes of those working in the beauty industry' by Réka Lukács-Márton, Eva Vásárhelyi and Pál Szabó (2008)

10 'Starvation Diets, Obsessive Training and No Plus-Size Models: Victoria's Secret sells a dangerous fantasy', date accessed 12/12/21, theguardian.com/lifeandstyle/2018/nov/22/victorias-secret-show-angels-lingerie

11 'Plump or corpulent? Lean or gaunt? Historical categories of bodily health in

nineteenth-century thought' by David J Hutson (2017)

12 'The Emergence of Overweight as a Disease Entity: Measuring up normality', Annemarie Jutel (2006)

13 'Body satisfaction, weight stigma, positivity, and happiness among Spanish adults with overweight and obesity' by Débora Godoy-Izquierdo, Juan González-Hernández, Alejandra Rodríguez-Tadeo, Raquel Lara, Adelaida Ogallar, Estefanía Navarrón, María J. Ramírez, Clara López-Mora and Félix Arbinaga (2020)

14 'Body fat, menarche, fitness and fertility' by Rose E Frisch (1987)

15 'Marketing in Communist-Ruled Cuba: From guerrilla to mainstream?', date accessed 12/12/21, reuters.com/article/us-cuba-marketing-idUSKCN0YM1IG

16 'How many ads do we see per day in 2021?', date accessed 12/12/21, ppcprotect.com/blog/strategy/how-many-ads-do-we-see-a-day

17 'Ancient coin dulls Cleopatra's beauty', date accessed 12/12/21, nbcnews.com/id/wbna17157862

18 'Beauty through history', date accessed 12/12/21, washingtonpost.com/archive/lifestyle/wellness/1987/01/27/beauty-through-history/301f7256-0f6b-403e-abec-f36c0a3ec313

19 'Women's idealised bodies have changed dramatically over time—but are standards becoming more unattainable?', date accessed 12/12/21, theconversation.com/womens-idealised-bodies-have-changed-dramatically-over

20 'The steel engraving lady', date accessed 12/12/21, americanwomenproject.weebly.com/the-steel-engraving-lady.html

21 'What men find attractive in different parts of the world', date accessed 12/12/21, thelist.com/40387/men-think-attractive-different-parts-world

22 'A Healthy Tan: Darker skin rated more attractive', date accessed 12/12/21, abcnews.go.com/Health/Wellness/tanning-study-shows-people-rated-hotter-darker-skin/story?id=12333040

23 'White and Beautiful: An examination of skin whitening practices and female empowerment in China' by Evelyn Yeung (2015)

24 *The State of Affairs: Rethinking infidelity* by Esther Perel (2019)

25 *The Way We Never Were* by Stephanie Coontz (1993)

26 *Sex Today in Wedded Life* by Edward Podolsky (1947)

27 'Promoting Healthy Body Image in College Men: An evaluation of a psychoeducation program' by Justin Henderson (2012)

28 *Ladies we need to talk* with Yumi Stynes, 'The gender beauty gap' (2020)

29 'The link between beauty and the gender gap', date accessed 12/12/21, forbes.com/sites/kimelsesser/2019/10/28/the-link-between-beauty-and-the-gender-gap

30 'Australia's gender pay gap statistics', date accessed 12/12/21, wgea.gov.au/publications/australias-gender-pay-gap-statistics

31 *We can do hard things* with Glennon Doyle, 'How to know ourselves and be known by our people' (2021)

32 'When Meditation turns Toxic: The woman exposing spiritual sexism', date accessed 10/12/21, theguardian.com/lifeandstyle/2021/dec/08/meditation-spirtual-sexism-womens-retreats

33 *Daily Telegraph,* quote by Anita Quigley (2006)

34 '4 ways our socially accepted beauty ideals are racist', date accessed 12/12/21, everydayfeminism.com/2017/05/beauty-ideals-racist

35 'Survey finds that 78% of models in fashion adverts are white', date accessed 10/12/21, theguardian.com/fashion/2016/may/10/survey-finds-that-78-of-models-in-fashion-adverts-are-white

36 'The last days of a white world', date accessed 12/12/21, theguardian.com/uk/2000/sep/03/race.world

37 'Do Ugly Criminals Receive Harsher Sentences? An analysis of lookism in the criminal justice system' by Kelly Beck (2010)

38 'The Dove Global Beauty and Confidence Report' by Dove (2016)

Part II

39 'Women's body confidence is a "critical issue" worldwide, warns Dove's largest ever report', date accessed 12/12/21, huffingtonpost.co.uk/entry/dove-global-body-image-report_uk_5762a6a1e4b0681487dcc470

40 'The importance of belonging', date accessed 12/12/21, edition.cnn.com/2012/06/01/health/enayati-importance-of-belonging/index.html

41 *What does Australia really think about obesity?* by SBS (2021)

42 '30% of Australia's population born overseas', date accessed 6/12/21 abs.gov.au/media-centre/media-releases/30-australias-population-born-overseas

43 'Racism study finds one in three school students are victims of discrimination', date accessed 6/12/21, theguardian.com/australia-news/2019/aug/27/racism-study-finds-one-in-three-school-students-are-victims-of-discrimination

44 'Terry Real: Fierce Intimacy', date accessed 25/2/22, resources.soundstrue.com/transcript/terry-real-fierce-intimacy

45 *The Beauty Suit* by Lauren Shields (2018)

46 'Why shaming doesn't work', date accessed 12/12/21, psychologytoday.com/us/blog/longing-nostalgia/201705/why-shaming-doesnt-work

47 'Body dysmorphic disorder', date accessed 6/12/21, mayoclinic.org/diseases-conditions/body-dysmorphic-disorder/symptoms-causes/syc-20353938

48 'Teen girls as avid shoppers', date accessed 6/12/21, adweek.com/brand-marketing/teen-girls-avid-shoppers-103813

49 'Fashion's environmental impacts', date accessed 6/12/21, sustainyourstyle.org/old-environmental-impacts

50 '30 shocking figures and facts in global textile and apparel industry', date accessed 12/12/21, business2community.com/fashion-beauty/30-shocking-figures-facts-global-textile-apparel-industry-01222057

51 'You'll be shocked by how long women spend on their hair and makeup each day', date accessed 12/12/21, womenshealthmag.com/beauty/a19954807/womens-beauty-routine

52 *Trick Mirror: Reflections on self-delusion* by Jia Tolentino (2019)

53 *The Beauty Myth* by Naomi Wolf (1990)

54 'Foot-binding', date accessed 12/12/21, worldhistory.org/foot-binding

55 'Cosmetic Surgery Market 2019: Global key players, trends, share, industry size, segmentation, opportunities, forecast to 2025', date accessed 12/12/21 medgadget.com/2019/10/cosmetic-surgery-market-2019-global-key-players-trends-share-industry-size-segmentation-opportunities-forecast-to-2025.html

56 'Risk and protective factors for perpetration', date accessed 12/12/21, cdc.gov/violenceprevention/intimatepartnerviolence/riskprotectivefactors.html

57 'Women who NEVER let even their husbands see them without make-up: The secret to a happy marriage—or sad proof of female insecurity?', date accessed 12/12/21 dailymail.co.uk/femail/article-3150249/The-women-NEVER-let-husbands-without-make-secret-happy-marriage-sad-proof-female-insecurity.html

58 'Prevalence and predictors of low sexual desire, sexually related personal distress, and hypoactive sexual desire dysfunction in a community-based sample of midlife women' by Roisin Worsley, Robin J Bell, Pragya Gartoulla and Susan R Davis (2017)

59 'Risks and complications of breast implants', date accessed 12/12/21 fda.gov/
medical-devices/breast-implants/risks-and-complications-breast-implants

60 '10 things you never knew about the clitoris', date accessed 12/12/21, health.com/
mind-body/10-things-you-never-knew-about-the-clitoris

Part III

61 'Kate Winslet's new contract bans retouching of her photos', date accessed 12/12/21,
hellomagazine.com/healthandbeauty/skincare-and-fragrances/2015102327855/kate-
winslet-will-no-longer-let-adverts-be-retouched

62 'What is Internal Family Systems?', date accessed 12/12/21, ifs-institute.com

63 'What is Imago Relationship Therapy?', date accessed 12/12/21, harvilleandhelen.
com/initiatives/what-is-imago

64 *Intimate Communion: Awakening Your Sexual Essence* by David Deida (2002)

65 'Do pheromones play a role in our sex lives?', date accessed 12/12/21,
scientificamerican.com/article/pheromones-sex-lives

66 'The surprising downsides of being drop dead gorgeous', date accessed 12/12/21,
bbc.com/future/article/20150213-the-downsides-of-being-beautiful

About the author

NICOLE MATHIESON

Nicole Mathieson has impacted the lives of thousands of women through her writing, speaking, podcasts and work as a counsellor.

In the therapy room, Nicole sees the Beauty Load doing its self-esteem-stealing damage in real time as she helps her clients grapple with not feeling good enough to love.

By sharing her own awkward stories and negative self-talk, Nicole inspires a deep exhale of recognition from her clients and readers alike, who, for possibly the first time, realise they are not alone, not crazy and absolutely not inadequate.

The Beauty Load is Nicole's first book.

CPSIA information can be obtained
at www.ICGtesting.com
Printed in the USA
LVHW051925290422
717576LV00004B/130

9 780645 344431